How to have
Healthy
Happy
Children
The 10-step plan

Kristina Murrin

BBC
ACTIVE

Contents

Introduction

Being a parent has many rewards, but mums and dads of this generation seem to be having a particularly difficult time. Not only are there an unprecedented amount of things to worry about, there also seems to be very little agreement about what's best for our children.

Ask two different 'experts' and you'll get two different replies – whether the topic is working mums or what to do about obese children. As a parent this lack of consensus can be very confusing.

No-one is taught how to be a parent. In order to drive a car we need to have lessons and pass a test – wouldn't it be great if we had a little support and guidance for the most important and fulfilling job in the world – bringing up children? Often, information we get has to be gleaned from friends, relatives, the media and other parents; much of which is often out of date or conflicting.

So how can we get on the right path with our children, at a time when levels of obesity, sleep deprivation, teenage pregnancy and other childhood problems have reached an all-time high? Rather than try to push a particular agenda or give you my own brand of parenting (and let's face it, as a mother of three I'm still learning), I've tried to sort the facts from the fiction when it comes to the issues surrounding parenting. I wanted to answer some of the common questions parents ask, such as, 'What constitutes a healthy diet?' or, 'How much exercise does my child need?' by digging out facts based on the best available science and research. Then, as a parent, you can go away and decide what to do with this knowledge. After all, you know your children better than anyone.

The following chapters look at diet, exercise, sleep, learning, love, getting involved, discipline, respect, safety and good communication. We know that there are certain factors that influence how long our children will live and how happy they'll be throughout their lifetimes – diet and exercise play a big part in this – but there also are some other factors you might not have thought of, such as how sociable your children are or how much sleep they get. Even the smallest changes in these areas can have immediate and long-lasting benefits for the whole family.

I'm really hoping that this book inspires you to adopt some simple principles and advice and adapt it to your own family. When it comes down to it, parents are role models: your children look to you to show them how the world works and how to behave in it, and they copy what you do. That's a great responsibility, but it's also a fantastic opportunity to bring the best out in your child. It's your job to teach them about life and guide them towards lifelong health, happiness and personal fulfilment. Good parenting starts with you.

chapter 1

Diet

A healthy diet is one of the most important gifts you can give your child. Not only is good food vital for optimum health, but children also need a wholesome diet to help them grow and develop. We all want what's best for our children, so why are we letting them eat such junk?

How healthy is your child's diet?

Unfortunately, a large proportion of young people don't eat balanced meals; only one in seven children in the UK has the recommended five portions of fruit and veg per day, while one in five is classed as obese. Today's children also consume twice as much salt as is healthy and put away an alarming average of half a kilo of sugary food per day.

Unhealthy diet, unhealthy children

Deceptively, whatever their diet, children often seem to have boundless energy and good health. However, children who eat huge amounts of processed food, snacks, sweets and fizzy drinks might look healthy on the outside, but what's going on inside their body is very different.

The main risk from a diet high in fat, sugar and salt is obesity. The proportion of children in the UK who are overweight or obese rose sharply in the 1980s and has continued to climb at a worrying rate. According to World Health Organization figures, the number of British children aged between two and four who are obese nearly doubled between 1989 and 1998. For those aged between six and 15, obesity rates grew even faster, trebling from 5 per cent to 16 per cent between 1990 and 2001 – that's almost one in every five children. And mums and dads are no better: the same study found that, overall, 52 per cent of mothers and 72 per cent of fathers were either overweight or obese.

Does it matter if your child is overweight?

Surely a little bit of 'puppy fat' is nothing to worry about in children? And haven't we got enough things to concern us on top of trying to keep our youngsters from scoffing junk food? Well, yes and no. While children need to feel loved and accepted for who they are and not what they look like, letting your child become overweight is not doing them any favours in the long term. Most children who are obese infants become obese adults – they never develop healthy eating habits. While obsessing about body image isn't, admittedly, healthy for a child, teaching your children about good food provides them with a vital tool that they should carry with them through into adulthood.

Obesity is tough for a child: someone who is overweight in childhood is twice as likely to die from heart disease when they reach adulthood, and fat children who become fat adults are more likely to suffer from high blood pressure and certain types of cancer.

But obesity in childhood can also have an effect on the here and now. The significant increase in numbers of children with diabetes has been largely attributed to rising levels of obesity, and fat children are more likely to have sleep disorders and psychological problems too, such as low self-esteem.

Not every child who eats badly is obese, but that doesn't mean that they won't be at risk from health problems. A child who is thin but eats a high-fat diet can still have an increased cholesterol level, which is a risk factor in heart disease. A diet that is deficient in vitamins A, C and E (the ones you get from fruit, veg and wholemeal bread) increases your child's risk of cancer and heart problems. Equally, too much salt can lead to raised blood pressure, which puts you at greater risk of heart attacks and strokes. The wrong diet can also affect the functioning of the major organs, can lower our immunity, and has been shown to encourage behavioural problems such as poor concentration and hyperactivity.

So, in fact, poor nutrition is responsible for adversely affecting many different areas of a child's mental and physical health and is thought to contribute to:

- Poor concentration.
- Mood swings and hyperactivity.
- Food cravings.
- Communication problems.
- Tiredness and irritability.
- Panic attacks and anxiety.
- Asthma and other allergies.
- Sleep problems.
- Learning difficulties.

On the other hand, research shows that a good diet helps a child to maintain a healthy weight, improves physical growth and protects against life-threatening illnesses. It can also help your child to do better academically by improving their concentration and general behaviour. It will even give them more energy during the day and help them to sleep better at night.

What children should be eating

It can be tough being a parent, especially when it comes to what you should feed your children. One minute we're told that children need lots of calcium from milk, for example, the next we're told to watch out for dairy allergies. It's the same with all sorts of foods and in recent years the number of food scares, such as salmonella, BSE, GM and pesticides, have exhausted parents to the point of utter confusion. So what should children really be eating?

For years now we have understood the basics of a healthy diet. *Whether you are an adult or a child, the advice is the same:* a balanced diet should contain a variety of food types, including:

- At least five portions of fruit and veg a day.
- Non-refined starchy foods, such as wholemeal bread and wholegrain cereals.
- Some protein-rich foods, such as meat, fish, eggs and lentils.
- Some dairy foods.

It's also important that food is freshly made and not processed because ready meals and junk food use lots of preservatives, have low vitamin and mineral levels and are high in fat and salt. (Fat and salt are cheap ways to make bland processed food taste better.)

Fruit and veg

If there's one thing that's key to you and your family's dietary health it's eating five portions of fruit and veg a day. It is the quickest way to help reduce the risk of some cancers and protect against heart disease. What's more, fruit and veg taste great and add variety to any meal. Eating five portions a day might sound a lot, but it's actually much easier than you think, especially when you see what counts as one portion (see opposite).

Starchy foods

Starchy foods are also an important part of a healthy diet. While you don't have to have them at every meal, current government guidelines suggest that starchy foods should make up about a third of the food that we eat overall. This is because they are a great source of energy and one of the main ways in which we get vital nutrients such as fibre, calcium, iron and some essential B vitamins.

In recent years, though, starchy foods have become unfashionable. Many weight-loss diets encourage us to avoid foods such as bread, but the reality is that they contain less than half the calories of fat. The problem arises when we add fat to our starchy foods – piling lots of butter on a jacket potato or adding margarine to toast – or when we eat only refined starchy foods such as white bread or white pasta.

The healthiest types of starchy food are the wholegrain options. White or refined starchy foods have had many of the important nutrients and fibre removed and should be avoided. Wholegrain foods, on the other hand, contain lots of fibre, which is vital for healthy digestion and for preventing bowel diseases. It also takes us longer to digest wholegrain foods, which means we are less likely to suffer from hunger pangs between meals. This is especially

Count to five

What counts as one portion of fruit and veg?

Green vegetables: 2 broccoli spears, 8 cauliflower florets, 4 heaped tablespoons of cabbage or green beans.

Cooked vegetables: 3 heaped tablespoons, such as carrots, peas or sweetcorn.

Salad vegetables: 3 sticks of celery, 5 cm cube of cucumber, 1 medium tomato, 7 cherry tomatoes.

Tinned/frozen vegetables: 3 heaped tablespoons of tinned or frozen carrots, peas or sweetcorn.

Pulses and beans: 3 heaped tablespoons of kidney, cannellini or butter beans, or chickpeas (beans or pulses can only count as one of your five-a-day portions).

Fresh fruit: 1 medium-sized fruit, such as 1 apple, banana, pear or orange.

Small-sized fruit: 2 plums, 2 satsumas, 2 kiwi fruit, 3 apricots, 7 strawberries, 14 cherries.

Large fruit: ½ grapefruit, 1 slice of melon (5 cm slice), 1 large slice of pineapple, 2 slices of mango (5 cm slice).

Dried fruit: 1 tablespoon of raisins, currants, sultanas, mixed fruit, 2 figs, 3 prunes.

Tinned fruit: 2 pear or peach halves, 6 apricot halves, 8 segments of tinned grapefruit.

Juice: 1 glass (150ml) of 100 per cent fruit juice (juice counts as only one portion a day, no matter how much you drink).

Source: Department of Health

important for children who tend to snack on junk food when they are feeling peckish.

Protein-rich foods

We all need to eat protein-rich foods. Protein is vital because it helps the body to repair itself, and it's doubly vital for children because protein also helps the body grow and develop. Lots of foods contain protein, including chicken, lean meat, fish, eggs and dairy products, and we should be aiming to get about 15 per cent of the calories we eat from these types of foods. Oily fish (such as salmon, mackerel and sardines) is an especially good source of protein as it contains lots of other beneficial nutrients including omega-3 fatty acids, which help keep our hearts healthy.* If you or your child is a vegetarian and these foods are not an option, don't worry: tofu, pulses and bread are also good sources of protein.

As a rough guide, men need about 50g and women need about 40g of protein a day. Children aged four to six need about 20g while those aged seven to ten need about 28g.

*Children should avoid eating any shark, swordfish or marlin. High levels of mercury in these fish can affect the development of the nervous system.

Dairy foods

Milk and other dairy products are a vital source of calcium, the mineral needed for your children to develop healthy

Healthy starchy foods

- Wholemeal, wholegrain and granary bread.
- Wholemeal pittas and chapattis.
- Wholewheat pasta.
- Brown rice.
- Wholegrain breakfast cereals.

Good protein sources

The average child needs between 20g and 28g of protein per day, depending on their age. This equates to the following:

- 1 chicken breast.
- 1 portion of lean Bolognese sauce.
- 1 small can of tuna, or 1 poached cod fillet.
- 1 cheese sandwich in wholemeal bread.
- 4–5 glasses of milk.
- 6 tablespoons of cooked red lentils.
- 1 serving of tofu.
- 6–9 slices of wholemeal bread.

bones and teeth. (A diet low in calcium can lead to osteoporosis.) Calcium is also important for muscle contraction, regulation of the heartbeat and the formation of blood clots. Dairy products are a vital source of protein and vitamins A, B12, and D, too.

If your child is allergic to cows' milk or has a lactose intolerance, it's very important for them to receive sufficient calcium from other foods. Tofu, tinned fish and green leafy vegetables are good sources, and there is also a number of products on the market now that have added calcium, such as orange juice and fortified cereals.

Milk

After weaning, children under two should drink only whole milk because they may not get enough calories from semi-skimmed milk. From two, semi-skimmed is fine, but skimmed milk is best avoided as it is very low in calories and contains only minute amounts of vitamins A and D. As a general guide, children between one and three need about 350mg of calcium a day – two glasses of full-fat milk will give them this.

Healthy dairy options for children

- Semi-skimmed milk for children over two years of age.
- Low-fat spread instead of butter.
- Cottage cheese, low-fat cream cheese, reduced-fat hard cheese.
- Low-fat fromage frais.
- Low-fat yoghurt.

Dairy foods and fat

While milk and dairy products are vital for children and adults, they also tend to contain a high percentage of fat. Although a certain amount of fat is essential for good health (see pages 19 and 22), it's important to limit your intake. Most children in the UK eat too much fat, so rather than cutting out dairy products – which contain other essential vitamins and nutrients – why not look for lower-fat versions of foodstuffs?

Vitamins, minerals and vegetarians

Our bodies need minute amounts of vitamins and minerals in order to function properly, and although the good news is that the majority of children and young people do receive adequate vitamins and minerals, a recent national survey found that there were a few notable exceptions:

- Older teenagers tend not to get enough vitamin A.
- More than a third of 11- to 14-year-old girls aren't getting enough zinc.
- Almost half of 11- to 14-year-old girls don't get enough iron.

Vegetarians also have to be careful that they are receiving an adequate intake of vitamins and minerals. Many children, especially teenagers, choose to eat a meat-free diet, so you need to ensure their meals are balanced and include all the necessary nutrients for growth and development. Give them foods such as milk, cheese and eggs so that their diet won't be too bulky and they'll get plenty of protein, vitamin A, calcium and zinc. Iron, which is often the nutrient most deficient in a meat-free diet, is also found in many vegetables and pulses (beans, lentils and chickpeas), in dried fruit (such as apricots, raisins and sultanas) and in some breakfast cereals.

A healthy balanced diet – whether vegetarian or not – should always include a variety of vitamins and minerals. If you are eating well, you shouldn't need to boost your diet with vitamin supplements. The chart on pages 20–1 helps you identify which are the key vitamins and minerals, why they are essential for children, and which foods contain a good supply.

What children are really eating

OK, we know what children should eat, but most parents will tell you the reality is very different.

It might be difficult to believe, but children actually ate more healthily in the 1950s than they do now. Research from University College, London, and the Medical Research Council found that despite food shortages in the post-war period, children in the fifties actually had a better intake of several key nutrients, including fibre, calcium, vitamins and iron, than they do today. This was because these children ate more bread and milk (increasing their fibre and calcium intake), drank fewer soft drinks (which meant less refined sugar), got lots of vitamin C from fresh vegetables and ate more red meat (giving them more iron).

So what are our children eating?

In comparison, modern children are missing out. Research shows that the foods most commonly consumed by youngsters in the UK are white bread, savoury snacks, crisps, biscuits, potatoes and chocolate. One in three people also eats a ready meal more than once a week (compared with only one in six in France). The problem with such a diet is that not only will a child who stuffs themselves with processed food and snacks be less likely to have room for fruit and vegetables, but they will also be consuming large amounts of fat, sugar and salt. A palate cultivated on artificially flavoured foods will find it difficult to adapt to the subtler tastes of fresh, healthy produce.

One in five children eats no fruit in a week, and three in five eat no leafy green vegetables.

The main offenders

Fat

Fat has a bad reputation. While a diet too high in fat can lead to specific health problems, a certain amount of fat in our diet keeps us healthy. The key to a balanced diet is knowing exactly how much fat you can safely consume and recognizing the difference between the various types of fats. Fat can be divided into two groups: saturated and unsaturated.

Saturated fats

These usually come from animal sources and are found in foods such as butter, cheese and lard. Saturated fat is also present in red meat. In general this type of fat is best avoided, as a diet too high in saturated fats can lead to obesity, heart disease and other health problems.

Unsaturated fats

In contrast, these fats usually come from vegetable sources. Oils made from foodstuffs such as olive, sunflower and soya all contain high levels of unsaturated fat, as do other foods such as oily fish and certain types of margarine. This type of fat is generally thought of as beneficial to health if eaten in moderation.

What vitamins and minerals do for your body

Vitamin A

Found in animal and vegetable sources. Helps to keep bones and teeth healthy. Also maintains good vision and promotes healthy skin. If you eat enough of these foods you can build an excellent immune system, which not only fights illnesses, but helps you recover from them as well.

Food sources

Apples, bananas, blackberries, blueberries, broccoli, cabbage, carrots, corn, grapes, green beans, kiwi, leeks, lettuce, nectarines, mangoes, oranges, parsley, passion fruit, peaches, pears, peas, peppers, pink grapefruits, plums, pumpkins, raspberries, sprouts, squash, strawberries, sweet potatoes, tomatoes, watercress.

Vitamin C

Needed for growth, healing of wounds and maintenance of bones and teeth. Foods rich in vitamin C are are excellent in preventing cancers of the lung, bladder, cervix and skin. The increased amount of lycopene in foods rich in vitamin C, such as tomatoes and grapefruits, can prevent bad sunburn and protect the skin.

Food sources

Apples, apricots, avocados, bananas, blueberries, broccoli, Brussels sprouts, cabbage, carrots, cauliflower, celery, corn, cranberries, cucumber, fennel, garlic, grapefruit, grapes, green beans, kiwi, leeks, lemons, lettuce, liver, melons, mushrooms, onions, oranges, papaya, parsley, pears, peas, pineapples, plums, potatoes, raspberries, spinach, strawberries, sweet potatoes, tomatoes.

Zinc

Aids food digestion, wound healing and physical growth. Eating foods containing zinc can help smell and taste functions, maintain a healthy metabolism and weight control and support healthy growth.

Food sources

Beans, dairy products, fortified breakfast cereals, green vegetables, lettuce, mushrooms, nuts, oysters, poultry, red meat, seafood, spinach, wholegrains.

Vitamin B

Provides energy to the body by converting sugars found in carbohydrate foods. B vitamins may help relieve some conditions such as depression and anxiety. The natural colourants in green vegetables can protect the eyes against cataracts, and protect the body from toxic substances that may cause infections. These foods also contain antioxidants.

Food sources

Brewer's yeast, brown rice, butter, cheese, eggs, fish, green vegetables, legumes, liver, meat, milk, peanuts, peas, potatoes, poultry, soya beans, wheat germ, wholegrain products.

Potassium

Usually found in plant-rich foods. Helps with muscle building, strength and functions of the nerves. Non-processed potassium-rich foods are best. Also, potatoes eaten with the skins on are more packed with potassium than without. When eaten on a regular basis, potassium may also help prevent weight gain and control water retention in the body.

Food sources

Apples, apricots, bananas, cherries, coconuts, dates, grapefruits, grapes, lemons, mangoes, melon, oranges, papaya, peaches, pineapple, raisins, raspberries, strawberries, tangerines.

Iron

Used to produce red blood cells in the body and usually comes from meat, cereals and pulses. Iron helps increase the body's red blood cell count and this in turn gives more energy and helps us exercise effectively and with vigour.

Food sources

Broccoli, Brussels sprouts, eggs, peas, red meat (lamb, beef, pork), salmon, sardines, spinach, wholegrain cereals, wholemeal bread.

The current UK government guidelines say that we should get no more than 35 per cent of our total energy intake from fat. (In America this figure is only 30 per cent.) For a woman, this means about 76g of fat per day, and for a man, this is roughly 100g. The problem is not only that adults and children are getting more like 40 per cent of their energy from fat (according to the National Diet and Nutrition Survey), but a large proportion of that fat is saturated, not unsaturated.

In the case of children, one of the big issues is that junk food and much of the food marketed directly at children is very high in saturated fat. Some frozen burgers, for example, contain meat that is 50 per cent fat, which means that a single portion has a whopping six teaspoons of fat – even if it's grilled! Other high-saturated-fat culprits include most take-away meals, such as fish and chips, kebabs, fried chicken, curries and pizzas.

Sugar

Children are born with a preference for sweet foods and have a natural dis-trust of bitter flavours. The scientific explanation is that sweetness signals that

How much fat is too much?

So how do you know whether a food is high in fat or not? If you look on the back of a packet it should tell you how many grams of fat per 100g it contains, but as a very general rule:

Very high-fat foods contain:
20g unsaturated fat or more per 100g.
5g saturated fat or more per 100g.

Very low-fat foods contain:
3g unsaturated fat or less per 100g.
1g saturated fat or less per 100g.

While you may struggle to eat only foods that count as **very low fat**, you can aim towards the recommended figure of getting no more than 35 per cent of your total energy from fat by avoiding the **higher-fat foods**.

To help you work out how much fat you should have per day, the current recommended daily limit is 100g for men and 76g for women. While there isn't a current recommended limit for children, it should clearly be less than either of these figures.

How much sugar is too much?

Sugar is the only foodstuff that is not actually needed by the body. For this reason there is no recommended daily intake, so instead the World Health Organization offers figures for the maximum intake. This quantity is no more than ten per cent of a child's total calorie intake per day coming from added sugar. Given that one teaspoon of sugar weighs 4g this equates roughly to:

- 11 teaspoons or 45g for children aged five to nine years.
- 12 teaspoons or 50g for children aged ten to 14 years old.
- 16 teaspoons or 65g for children aged 15 and over.

Remember that this maximum amount doesn't just include teaspoons of sugar added to drinks, but also includes the sugar content of all sugary foods such as sweets, cakes and fizzy drinks. For example:

- One can of Coke contains 9 tea spoons or 35g of sugar.
- 100g of Kellogg's Frosties contains 9 teaspoons or 38g of sugar.
- 100g of Sugar Puffs contains 12 teaspoons or 49g of sugar.

a food is full of calories, while bitterness signals the possibility of poison. In moderation, sugar does little or no harm; however, excessive consumption can lead to obesity and tooth decay (see Tooth decay on pages 24–5). Although the research has thus far proved inconclusive, many parents and teachers also believe that sugar has adverse effects on children's behaviour, encouraging hyperactivity or energy swings.

Children aged between seven and ten years old consume, on average, more than half a kilo of sugary food every day. The worst offenders are soft drinks – a standard can of cola, for example, contains a staggering nine teaspoons of sugar (35g) – and energy drinks are even worse. Other high-sugar foods include flavoured yoghurts, sugary breakfast cereals, cakes, biscuits, sweets, chocolate, puddings and ice cream.

Sugar cravings

The body often yearns for sugar, but there are ways to control sugar cravings. To do this, you need to know more about 'good' and 'bad' types of sugar.

Hot topic Tooth decay

What is it?

Dental decay is a breakdown of the normal hard tissues on the outer surface of the teeth to form a soft cavity or hole. In severe decay, the cavity may be very deep, affecting the nerve and blood vessels.

What causes it?

The bacteria that thrive on the teeth are responsible for decay, particularly when there's a large amount of sugary food debris left in the mouth. These bacteria grow in a sticky coating on the teeth called plaque. They break down these food sugars into acids that etch away at the surface enamel. Frequent consumption of sugary foods and drinks increases the risk of decay, especially if they are allowed to surround the teeth for long periods of time (for example, if teeth aren't regularly brushed or if a baby sucks on a bottle full of sweet drink).

How do sugars attack your teeth?

Invisible germs live in your mouth all the time and some of these form plaque on the surface of the teeth. When you put sugar in your mouth, the bacteria in the plaque gobble up the sweet stuff and turn it into acids. These acids dissolve the hard enamel that covers your teeth, allowing the calcium and phosphate minerals to leak out, and softening and destroying the enamel and dentine below. That's how cavities get started. If you restrict your sugar intake, the bacteria can't produce as much of this acid.

Who's affected?

Dental decay is very common. The addition of fluoride to toothpaste has helped to protect teeth and reduce decay, but the continuing trend towards sweeter snacks in children's diets is working against these precautions.

At first, tooth decay may not cause any obvious symptoms – especially in milk teeth – but as it progresses it may cause toothache, or sensitivity to hot

or cold or very sweet foods. If the nerve becomes affected, an infection may establish and lead to an abscess, which brings with it severe pain, swelling of the jaw and fever.

What can I do to prevent my child getting tooth decay?

- Limit your child's intake of sugary food and drinks.
- Discourage grazing – snacking on sugary treats is actually worse than eating all your sweets in one go.
- Set a good example yourself.
- Think about what you buy – check the food labels for added sugar.
- Make sure your children clean their teeth regularly every morning and evening and after a sugary snack.

'Bad' sugars – simple sugars and highly refined grains in foods such as white flour, sweets and cakes – cause your child's blood sugar level to rise extremely quickly and then slump, with an associated mood change. Complex natural sugars, or 'good' sugars, are broken down more slowly, allowing blood sugar levels to rise more gradually; these are found in fruit and wholewheat products.

So how do you make the swap from bad to good? The key is to make sure that the majority of sugar in your child's diet is the complex natural kind, while limiting the amount of added sugar – by cutting down on soft drinks, sweets and so on. You need to start healthy habits as early as possible with your children, but the good news is that these habits will stay with them for the rest of their life.

Salt

Most children eat twice as much salt as the recommended daily allowance (see below). The problem is that salt is often hidden in the food that children like the most – one take-away burger, for example, will give a young child more salt than his total daily allowance. Similarly, bread, pizzas, sausages, tinned spaghetti, soups and baked beans can often contain too much, while lunchbox favourites such as processed cheese, sliced meats and savoury snacks also tend to be high in salt. Surprisingly, even sweet products such as breakfast cereals, biscuits and hot chocolate can contain large amounts of salt.

To make matters worse, many foods have actually got saltier over the past few decades. Between the years of 1978 and 2003, for example, the average salt content in a packet of crisps has doubled.

Eating too much salt can raise your blood pressure, thus tripling your chance of heart disease, whatever your age.

How much salt is too much?

These are the current guidelines for children's salt intake per day – bear in mind that one teaspoon is the equivalent of 6g of salt. But be warned that salt is also present in food as 'sodium', which is 2.5 times more concentrated than salt. If you read a label saying '1.2g sodium', it actually contains about 3g salt.

- 1 to 3 years – 2g salt (0.8g sodium)
- 4 to 6 years – 3g salt (1.2g sodium)
- 7 to 10 years – 5g salt (2g sodium)
- 11 and over – 6g salt (2.5g sodium)

Foods that are high in salt include:

- Bacon
- Baked beans (look for low-salt versions instead)
- Biscuits
- Chips
- Crisps and other salty snacks
- Fast food, including burgers and pizzas
- Fish in brine
- Gravy granules
- Ready-made cooking sauces and ready meals
- Sausages
- Smoked meat and fish
- Soy sauce, stock cubes and yeast extract
- Tinned pasta, e.g. spaghetti hoops
- Tinned soup
- Tinned vegetables (with added salt)

Common barriers to healthy eating

Many parents would dearly love their children to eat a healthy diet but often find themselves running into difficulties. At the end of this chapter you'll find some general tips to help your child eat more healthily, but first let's take a look at some of the specific reasons why children have an unhealthy diet – and, more to the point, what you can do about it.

Fussy eaters

Food fads are surprisingly common. In fact, two thirds of children go through a stage of refusing to eat certain foods, especially between the ages of two and ten. Sometimes this is because children genuinely dislike the taste of a particular food, whereas for others fussy eating is a normal part of a child's growing sense of independence and choice. After all, adults don't like all foods, so why should we expect our children to?

Occasionally there are more complex issues behind selective eating. Young children generally have little control over their life and food is one of the few arenas in which they can express themselves. Refusing to eat can be a way of showing anger, anxiety or need for attention, as well as gaining control.

Fussy eating is almost always more distressing for the parent than for the child. When your child refuses food it can feel like a rejection of your effort and love. Children are canny observers and they can sense these feelings, which may encourage them to do it even more. But there are a lot of things you can do if your child will eat only a narrow range of foods. (See page 28.)

Tight budget

Some parents resist giving their children healthy food because they think it will cost more. However, the picture isn't as straightforward as it would first appear. While certain healthier foods sometimes carry a heftier price tag – for example, organic or biodynamic – many healthy foods cost the same as or even less than unhealthy meals. Ready meals, processed food and take-aways are often more expensive than fresh food, comparatively, because you are paying someone to make the meal, in addition to covering their raw material costs.

So it doesn't have to cost more to eat healthily; you just need to plan a little. See page 29 for some tips on how to have a healthy diet on a budget.

Top tips for fussy eaters

Don't panic

Maintain a low-key approach when offering any food. Many experts suggest putting the food on the table and encouraging just one bite, and not reacting positively or negatively whether the child likes it or not. Above all, stay calm if your child refuses to eat something, and don't insist on a clean plate.

No bribes

When kids are cajoled into eating a food or even rewarded or praised for eating it, the child often develops an aversion to that particular food. Try not to offer foods as rewards or say 'There's no pudding until you've eaten all those vegetables.' By doing so you are simply reinforcing the idea that the pudding is more desirable than the vegetables.

Out with the junk

Pack the refrigerator and the cupboards with healthy foods, put only balanced meals on the table and keep all other undesirable foods out of the house. It's best to keep less healthy food away from temptation, and then bring it in on special occasions when you let the children have control over eating it.

One at a time

When it comes to new foods, offer only one at a time, and remeber that children are more likely to try a new food if they have the option of not swallowing it.

Hide the veg

If your child has an aversion to veg, try putting them in a cheese sauce or blending them in a soup. Children also like to eat them when they are fresh and crispy, so try offering crudités – clean, crisp, fresh vegetables cut into strips to be eaten with fingers – with a yoghurt dip, for example. You could even try giving them vegetable juices such as carrot or tomato juice.

Eat together

Believe it or not, most children like eating with their parents, so try to eat something yourself with your children, even if you are planning a meal later. Children sometimes accept small tastes of alternatives from somebody else's plate – it's less overwhelming than the sight of a food they don't like in front of them.

Eating healthily without breaking the bank

■ If you shop at the end of the day, you'll often find that perishable foods such as bread, meat and veg are reduced in price.

■ Fruit and veg in season are cheaper and usually contain fewer pesticides: for example, satsumas in winter, cherry tomatoes in summer.

■ Avoid bags of pre-made salad – individual lettuces will go further, last longer and cost less.

■ Buy lean meat. It might be a little more expensive, but there's less waste and less fat.

■ Oily fish such as mackerel, herring and sardines are cheaper than other varieties, but just as good for you.

■ Frozen and tinned fruit and veg are usually cheaper and allow you to use what you need and store the rest. You might not realize, too, that frozen vegetables also contains the same vitamin and mineral levels as fresh.

■ Wholegrain and wholemeal starchy foods, such as brown rice and wholemeal bread, are filling, cheap and nutritious.

■ Buy economy and own-label brands for basic items like tinned tomatoes; they're always cheaper and usually just as good.

■ Plan your shopping before you go. Make a list, but be flexible if a good offer turns up. Be wary of gimmicks: end-of-aisle displays are not always special offers.

■ Make a few portions of meals at once and freeze them. It's the cheapest and most time-efficient way of cooking.

School dinners and snacks

Many parents say that they try to feed their children healthy food but their attempts are ruined by the fact that school dinners are so awful, and because their children are snacking during the day when out of sight of mum and dad.

Many children have returned to the good old days of taking their own packed lunches. In fact, nine out of ten children now take a packed lunch to school. So surely a meal prepared by parents will be healthier than a school dinner? Well, not necessarily.

A recent study by the Food Standards Agency found that parents were packing their children off to school with lunchboxes filled with saturated

Top tips for school lunchboxes

- Keep it varied and interesting. Don't go for sandwiches every time – bagels, baps, wraps and pitta breads are great alternatives.
- Prevent bread from being too dry by using low-fat mayo, light cream cheese or a drizzle of yoghurt instead of butter.

- Swap fizzy sugary drinks for real fruit juice, semi-skimmed milk, mineral water or low-sugar cordial.
- Children love tiny treats – mini boxes of sultanas, a flapjack, yoghurt-covered raisins or a little tub of fruit salad will go down well.

fat, sugar and salt. The study revealed that the average lunchbox contained double the recommended lunchtime intake of saturated fat and sugar, and half the total daily recommended intake of salt. Foods such as crisps, fatty spreads, cheese products, chocolate bars and biscuits were to blame for the high levels

of saturated fat; white bread, crisps and processed meats explained the high salt intake; while fruit squashes, chocolate-covered bars, biscuits and yoghurts sent sugar levels sky-high. Three out of four lunchboxes failed to meet government nutritional standards for school meals, less than a fifth of lunchboxes (16 per cent) did not contain starchy food such as sandwiches, pasta or rice, and half the lunchboxes

A typical school lunchbox contains double the recommended intake of saturated fat, and sugar.

Source: Food Standards Agency

(48 per cent) lacked even a single portion of fruit or veg. See the box on page 30 for ideas on what to give your child at lunchtime.

Family meals

If a family doesn't eat together it can often be difficult to know whether your children are eating healthily or not. A recent Gallup poll found that a quarter of all children in the UK eat their evening meal off a tray sitting in front of the telly. Even more worryingly, *Mother & Baby* magazine's 'Feeding the Family' survey

Getting the family to eat together

■ Don't set rigid, unachievable goals. If eating together every day is almost impossible, set a target of three to four meals a week.

■ Turn the TV off to ensure quality time for conversations.

■ Have some guidelines, such as no fighting or teasing.

■ Try not to control conversations or suppress children's opinions at the table.

■ Anticipate work and school activities that may affect the timing of meals.

■ If you're not used to eating together it may be difficult at first and conversation may be slow. Persevere, and it will undoubtedly get easier.

■ If you think the children would enjoy it, get them involved in making the dinner. Depending on their age, they could help with the cooking, preparing ingredients, setting the table and so on.

Kris's Top Tips

Set a good example

It's no use trying to get your kids to eat healthily if you don't yourself. Children learn their eating habits from their parents, so it's vital that you set a good example.

Love good food

Healthy eating shouldn't be miserable. Encourage your kids to develop an interest in good food – take them to markets and delicatessens, try new and exciting cuisines from different cultures, teach them to care about where their food comes from and buy them cookbooks. Learning to appreciate food will help them to reject the artificial flavours of processed food.

Reclaim family mealtimes

Eating together as a family is one of the most important ways to change your child's eating habits.

Teach your children to cook

Getting older children involved in the actual cooking of family meals is not only a great way of encouraging them to help out around the house, but it also teaches them a valuable life skill for the future. Younger children can help out too – there are lots of great no-cook recipes, such as fruit salads, smoothies and sandwiches.

Don't sweat about the small stuff

It's much more important to get your child's overall diet sorted than to focus on the odd unhealthy snack. The main tasks should be getting your children to eat five portions of fruit and veg a day, increasing their consumption of all the vital nutrients and vitamins, and cutting down on the junk.

Know your food labels

Look out for the fat, sugar and salt content on packets and tins, and keep an eye on additives and E-numbers.

Be wary of 'children's food'

Don't assume that just because a food product is aimed at children it'll be healthy. These foods are often low in essential nutrients but high in fat, salt and sugar, relying on artificial colourings and flavourings for their appeal.

Keep an eye on TV-watching habits

Spending too long in front of the telly can fuel a child's desire for junk food by exposing them to adverts – cartoon characters and superheroes in particular are used to help sell nutritionally poor food to children. A child who watches lots of TV also gets less exercise and, if he or she eats in front of it, has a greater risk of over-eating.

Establish good habits as early as possible

Good eating habits should begin as soon as possible. Getting your child hooked on junk food will strengthen their preference for it, while getting them used to fresh food at an early age should have the opposite effect.

Keep it in perspective

Changing your child's diet won't happen overnight and you may have the occasional battle on your hands. The key is to keep a sense of perspective and remain calm.

in 2004 discovered that 48 per cent of all toddlers eat on their own in front of the TV, rather than at the table with the rest of the family.

This is bad news for three reasons. First, because research has shown that people who eat whilst sitting in front of the television tend to have a higher calorie intake than those who sit at the table. (This is because you are too distracted to notice whether you are feeling full.) Second, adverts shown during children's television are often for junk food and sweets, making them more appealing to young appetites. And finally, because it's a missed opportunity, the evening meal is probably one of the best, and only, times for a family to sit down and socialize together. For young children this is especially important as sitting with other people and seeing them eat a variety of foods encourages the child to want to try different food too.

chapter 2

Exercise

If you're tired, stressed and busy, it can seem a blessed relief if your children will play computer games or gaze at the TV for hours. Unfortunately, while it can be tempting to let them be couch-potatoes, lack of physical activity is bad news for their health, development and wellbeing – and you're missing out on a brilliant way to have fun as a family.

How much exercise are your children getting?

Let's start with a basic principle. Child health experts agree that children need one hour of moderate physical exercise every day but, unfortunately, the reality is very different. Did you know that the average teenager takes less exercise than the average pensioner? In Britain, one third of all boys and one half of all girls get less than the recommended one hour of exercise a day. Put simply, around 40 per cent of children aren't getting enough exercise.

So why is this? And, in particular, why are children in the UK getting so little exercise compared with previous generations? These are some of the reasons:

Transport

We are a nation of car owners. Three-quarters of households in the UK now own at least one car, while one in 20 families has three or more vehicles. While cars have transformed our life and made us freer in many ways, they've also made us much lazier – a recent survey found that over a fifth of all car journeys are less than a mile long.

An internet census of 50,000 primary school children revealed that 50 per cent of them are chauffeured to and from school by car.

Source: Qualifications & Curriculum Authority

School journeys

An offshoot of car ownership has been the increase in people participating in what we all call the 'school run'. While in previous years the journey to and from school was a good opportunity for children to walk or cycle, many children are now driven there and back. This is an opportunity missed and a real shame; a recent study in the British county of Hertfordshire showed that while walking to school each day, Year 8 pupils use more calories than during the two hours of PE they receive each week.

Road safety

Ironically, parents state that one of the reasons they don't let their children walk or cycle to school is fear of them being knocked over by a car. As a result, more children are driven to school, which puts more cars on the road, so they are even more unsafe. There is also evidence that children who are driven have more road accidents as teenagers because they have undeveloped road awareness.

Parents' fears

Parents today don't just worry about their children being involved in a road accident; they are also terrified that all sorts of dangers await them in the outside world. Thus many parents are frightened to let their children play in the street or in the park, and prefer them to stay cooped up at home. Many experts believe these fears are greater than they should be – partly as a result of exaggeration in the media – but these fears are also understandable.

Statistically, a sedentary lifestyle is more of a risk to a child's health than any random act of violence by a stranger. The incidence of children being abducted and killed by a stranger is low – less than five out of 16 million children per year in the UK. (Children are statistically safer today than in their parents' generation.) Poor nutrition and lack of exercise, on the other hand, are almost guaranteed to shorten your life. Current estimates published in the *New England Journal of Medicine* warn that obesity can cut an individual's life expectancy by between five and 20 years.

Decline of school sport

In the last 30 years, sport has simply not been given the priority that it deserves in the agenda of British schools, and as a result the amount of teaching time devoted to it has declined massively. In 1970 children took part in an average of five hours of sport at school per week: today the average is just over one and a half hours. School playing fields are also disappearing at an alarming rate, as schools raise funds by selling off valuable land to property developers. The upshot is that now we have a generation of children for whom sport is more often a spectator event than an everyday activity. Thankfully, there are signs that the government is beginning to recognize this problem and is finally placing more emphasis on the importance of school sport.

Technology

A major contributory factor to the problem of lack of exercise, this reason almost goes without saying. Although they can, in some instances, be informative and entertaining for children, video and television games are incredibly addictive and prevent children from regulating their own play in a healthy way. Today's busy parents, who are often away from home a considerable amount, contribute to this problem by not being present to monitor TV and game time. As a result, children sit in front of the TV for far too long, getting no exercise while they do so. Current statistics, for example, suggest that the average teenager watches between 2.5 and 3.2 hours of TV every single day – and that doesn't include time spent playing computer games or watching DVDs.

Why do children need exercise?

Insufficient exercise leads to numerous problems in later life, but let's start with an increasingly common problem – obesity. Obesity is primarily caused by two things: poor diet, which we looked at in Chapter 1, and lack of exercise. Obesity in childhood contributes to the following:

- Increased pressure on joints.
- Reduced energy.
- Low self-esteem.
- Lack of self-confidence.
- Anxiety and depression.
- Serious health conditions, such as diabetes.

Studies of school children show that attendance figures and attentiveness rise when children take regular exercise, while exclusions and disruptive behaviour fall.

Source: Qualifications & Curriculum Authority

But perhaps the biggest danger of obesity in childhood is that fat children are much more likely to become fat adults. The older we get, the harder it usually is to lose weight and stay at a healthy weight.

Exercise (in conjunction with a healthy diet) is the best way to address excess weight. Weight is gained if you regularly eat more calories than you burn off, so it's a simple equation: children need to balance their energy intake and output.

Even if your children aren't obese, lack of exercise early on can contribute to a huge array of problems later in life, including heart disease, strokes, colon cancer, diabetes, hypertension and premature death. To illustrate the point, here's a fact that might surprise you. The British Heart Foundation states that the biggest single risk factor in developing heart disease isn't diet, obesity or smoking (although all of those are dangerous enough); it's a lack of physical activity. Help your children to enjoy exercise and they'll keep doing it through-out their life, so reducing their risk of contracting these deadly illnesses.

Think positive

All of this might sound very scary – and the potential problems caused by lack of exercise are certainly extremely serious – but if you are someone who responds better to optimism than fear, remind yourself of the enormous range of benefits that exercise has for children. Here are the important ones:

Physical self-confidence

Sport can improve balance, strength, coordination, concentration and flex-ibility, so children who exercise regularly are usually far more confident when faced with new tasks – everything from driving to cooking.

Sociability

Sport is a great way for all children – especially shy ones – to make new friends and teaches them important principles such as teamwork and cooperation.

Competitiveness and ambition

Life isn't all about competition, but competing is certainly a part of life. An ability to enjoy competition and to have a determination to succeed benefits children enormously, both in childhood and adult life. Competitive sport will encourage both these attributes.

Emotional wellbeing

Physical health has a positive impact on mental health. It can help fight off anxiety, depression and low self-esteem – three of the most common emo-tional problems suffered by children.

Better sleep patterns

Children who exercise use up excess energy during the day, and so tend to get to sleep more easily and have deeper sleep than those who don't.

Here's something else worth thinking about. In a recent survey, nine out of ten children said that they thought exercising was a good thing. So it's not as though children don't want to exercise these days – they really are interested in being active and keeping fit, but it seems that there are too many distractions. Another reason for their supposed apathy is, perhaps, that children aren't given the opportunities to do the things that they'd really like to. And this is where you can make a real difference.

Are your children getting their hour per day?

So how much exercise do your children get? Lots of parents have a vague idea of how much junk food their children eat and how long they spend in front of the TV, but have you ever stopped to work out how much exercise they get each week? If the answer is no, it's something you need to find out now and keep an eye on.

It's fairly easy to work out approximately how much exercise a child is getting; you'll have to ask them how many activities they are involved with away from home or at school, but you can keep a note of what they do in or around the house.

At the end of the week, make a note of the difference between how much exercise your children actually get and how much they should be getting (one hour a day). This way you'll be able to see whether they are on target. If they're not, it's time to start making some changes.

Let's get active!

So it's simple: children need at least one hour of exercise a day. But here's the good news – that doesn't mean that they have to do a full hour of sport every day. The following activities are just as beneficial:

A brisk walk – for example, to school or back, to the shops, or to see a friend.

Energetic playground activity – playing football, tag, hopscotch or skipping.

Time spent playing active games – either in the back garden or in the park (such as playing tag with brothers and sisters, or football).

A cycle ride – round to see a friend, or in the park.

Role models

Imagine that you're standing at the fitness section in the video shop wondering which workout video to buy for yourself. Which one would you buy – the one with the fit, slim trainer with muscles in all the right places, or the one who's overweight, sitting on a sofa, and looks like they last went for a run in 1985?

Now think about that in relation to your children and how they view exercise. You keep telling them to get out and about, but when did you last go for a run or play a game of squash? One of the most important principles to bear in mind regarding children and exercise is that they look to you for an example. If you take regular exercise they are more likely to; if you play team sport they are more likely to join in too.

It doesn't matter if you're just not the sporty type. Don't worry if you weren't much good at sport at school, or you have a disability of some sort – there are always ways to make sure you get exercise. Take a walk to the top of the hill and back every day, go out and do a bit of gardening regularly, or walk the dog. By getting out there you'll be doing something for yourself, but you'll also be setting a vital example to your children.

Perhaps you had some unhappy experiences whilst playing sport or exercising when you were younger? Perhaps a teacher or coach was too hard on you, or maybe you suffered some painful injuries? Or maybe you just didn't enjoy sport. Whatever your reasons, it's really important that you don't let these negative feelings prevent your children getting into exercise. Be enthusiastic, and you never know – you might find yourself enjoying an activity now that you didn't like when you were younger.

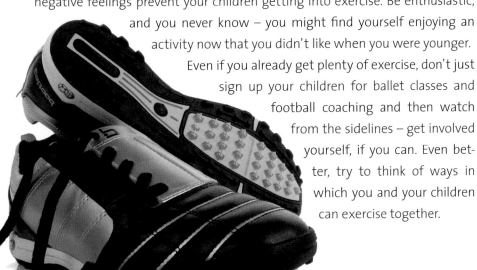

Even if you already get plenty of exercise, don't just sign up your children for ballet classes and football coaching and then watch from the sidelines – get involved yourself, if you can. Even better, try to think of ways in which you and your children can exercise together.

Sporting heroes

How many children have wanted to become a pop star after seeing their favourite singer on TV? Well, the same is true of sport: children love role models and heroes.

The recent success of the England cricket team is a good example. Back in 1981, when Ian Botham beat Australia almost single-handedly, an entire nation of UK school children was enthralled and, as a result, the numbers of children taking up cricket in the following couple of years soared. In 2005, with England winning the Ashes for the first time in 18 years, the same thing is happening again. In many places throughout England, cricket clubs are reporting a 100 per cent rise in new child members – all of them wanting to be the next cricketing superstar.

If your child asks you one day if they can have a poster of their favourite sporting hero, by all means buy them one, but don't stop there – ask them if they'd like to join a local sports team, too. Encouraging children to follow a hero is a brilliant way to get them enthusiastic about sport.

Sporting events

Taking your children to see sporting events is a wonderful way to introduce them to sport and exercise. Sport on TV is fine, but it is nowhere near as exciting as going to see it live – let them soak up the atmosphere at a football or cricket match, or the excitement at a motor race, to name just a few examples. Children are far more inspired by seeing sportsmen and women performing up close than on the TV.

However, it doesn't just have to be something obvious such as taking them to see a football match. What about a major athletics event or, if they like horses, how about showjumping? Be imaginative and try lots of events to see which ones your children enjoy the most. Whatever the sport, it'll be a brilliant outing for the family, something totally different from what you usually do and, you never know, it might really inspire your children to take up a sport.

Use your enthusiasm

Which sports do you enjoy? Athletics, a game of cricket, or perhaps something more graceful such as ice skating? Whatever sport or activity you're thinking of getting your children involved in, showing enthusiasm for it is one of the best ways to get them interested. It's the same with food – show them that you enjoy eating healthy food and they're much more likely to enjoy it too. Of course, the sports and activities that you're most likely to show enthusiasm for are usually the ones that you enjoy yourself.

Joint activities

If you've never done much exercise with your children, there are enormous benefits you might have never thought of. For instance:

Safety If you worry a lot about your child's safety, or perhaps if you live in an area where it's not safe for your children to play outside, taking part in activities with them is an excellent way of getting your children to exercise while also being able to keep an eye on them.

Shy children If your children are shy, or lack confidence, exercising with them will help to introduce them gently to physical activity and the outdoors, without them feeling they're on their own.

Bonding Playing together helps you bond with your children. You may find you spend a huge amount of time telling them what to do and what not to do, but having fun as a family is really important and if you take time to do it, they'll feel that you understand them better.

Sociability If it's difficult for your children to play with others because of where they live, joining in with them might well be one of the only ways you'll be able to get them to exercise. Children who don't live close to friends often don't want to go out on their own to the park or to a sporting event – it's just no fun having no-one to play with.

Finding sports in your area

Not sure where to start when it comes to finding sports for your children to do in the local area? It's actually much easier than you think.

School

One of the best places to start is at your child's local school. Despite the decline in the hours each week that are dedicated to PE in most schools, after-school sports clubs are still thriving. Not only do these offer a great opportunity for your child to be involved in team sports, but you can also feel confident that the activities are supervised by a responsible adult. School sports foster friendships between children while also helping to develop a feeling of pride, both of which are hugely beneficial for any child.

Parents can get involved with their child's school sports in lots of ways. There's a reliable body of data that suggests that the more practical support and encouragement parents, siblings and friends provide, the more likely they are to get involved in, and keep up with, a sport. Depending on the level of involvement that your child feels comfortable with (and it must be their choice), you can cheer from the sidelines, coach a team, make the half-time teas or simply offer your services as a taxi to take the children to home or away games. Even if they don't want you present at the games, you can still provide support in the form of washing their sports kit, altering meal times to accommodate fixtures and taking an interest in their game.

Sometimes schools organize sports-based trips. Despite the fact that school trips have received bad press in the past few years (see Chapter 9 on Safety for more information), school outings are still one of the safest ways for your child to be involved in sport. If at all possible, allow your child to go on these trips – whether it's a week's skiing or a weekend outward-bound course. Children almost invariably get a lot out of these trips in terms of confidence, exercise and independence.

Sports centres and gyms

If your child fancies a sport that isn't connected to their school, why not check out what facilities or instruction are offered by the local authority? Your local sports centre is a great place to start and will often have events specially designed for children to take part in. To find out what's going on in your area, contact your local council, which is responsible for running all the public sports centres in your area. If you have access to a computer, you can search for local facilities by going on to your city council website – it's usually the name

How to teach your child to ride a bike

Research among children who cycle has shown that wearing a helmet reduces the risk of head injury by 63 per cent and the risk of losing consciousness by 86 per cent. In other words, you can actually alter your child's chances of being seriously injured by making them wear a safety helmet.

■ Always make sure that your child **cycles safely** and with care and attention to everything that is happening around them.

■ Always ensure they wear a **helmet**, along with protective pads for knees and elbows. These pads can be removed once the child is confident of their cycling ability, but the helmet must always be worn.

■ Always choose a flat area of land **away from dangers** such as broken glass, uneven gravel paths, broken posts and objects sticking out of the ground.

■ Check that the area you have chosen has a lot of **forward-facing space** for your child to get their bearings and balance.

■ Put your child on the bike and hold on to one handlebar and the back of their sweatshirt (like a handle). Have the child begin to pedal while you help steer. Your child will feel the wobble of the bike, and you shouldn't try to prevent this as they will learn to balance using the wobble as a guide. Reassure the child that you are there with them and will stay right there.

■ After a few lessons, let go of the handlebar (you, not the child!), and hold on to the back of their sweatshirt only. This gives them new sense of freedom, and within a short period of time you won't even have to hold on to their sweatshirt.

■ This will not be a skill that they learn overnight. It is likely to be highly frustrating for both parents and children. Then, one day, off they go, riding a two-wheeled bike as if they were born on it!

■ NB – Falling is a fact of life: reassure your child that falls will happen, but they are part of the learning process. Understanding this, your child will soon be a confident cyclist.

Hot topic Sporty and unsporty children

What if your child is simply not sporty?

Time to explode a common myth. There is no such thing as an 'unsporty' child. Usually, if a child is persistently shying away from exercise, it's either because the conditions aren't right (for example, they're in a place or with people they don't like), or because they're not playing the right sport for them. There is a sport or activity to suit every child, so experiment to find the right one for your child.

The health implications of exercise are too important to let your children do nothing. You need to find ways to get your child to enjoy exercise, even if they do seem to be the indoors type.

The non-competitive child

Many individuals might not necessarily take to the competitive side of sport, and there are as many reasons why. Encourage your child to do well, but don't push them too hard – if they're not enjoying something, they're less likely to continue doing it later in life. If you're playing a sport against your child, make sure they can experience the genuine thrill of winning. Give yourself a points handicap and give your child a bit of a chance.

Don't feel as passionate as them about their sport of choice?

Unfortunately, it's bad luck for you. You must encourage your children in whichever sport they choose, even if it's not something that you yourself would enjoy.

Fear that a child will not excel at a chosen sport

This thought crosses the minds of many parents when their child expresses an interest in sport – especially something with quite distinct physical associations, such as rugby, martial arts, or even ballet. It is vital that you keep any doubts about their ability to yourself.

Remember that, although some challenges can seem daunting, it can give a child an amazing confidence boost to achieve something they're passionate about, despite the odds. So, have confidence in them and believe they can do well, whatever your immediate feelings are. Don't underestimate them, or their determination to succeed. Let them find out for themselves whether or not an activity is right for them.

of your town or city followed by .gov.uk (for example, the site for Southampton City Council is www.southampton.gov.uk). Alternatively, you can search through the local phone book, which will list all the sports centres in your area. The great thing about local authority sports centres is that they represent good value for money and, in many cases, will charge only minimal fees for children's sports. Your child will also get the opportunity to mix with a fantastic range of children.

If you're a member of a private gym, why not ask whether they have activities for children? Young people often get discounted rates for joining, or you could think about a family membership. Private gyms often have kids' clubs, too, which offer supervised physical activities for your children to enjoy while you exercise elsewhere without worrying about keeping an eye on them.

Sports clubs

There are lots of websites that will help you to locate a sports club in your area (see Further resources). If you have a specific sport in mind, say football or swimming, most sports have a professional association which can help you locate your nearest club.

If you want to get involved too, consider becoming a sports volunteer. Local clubs are always on the lookout for unpaid help – in fact, nearly 1.5 million people are sports volunteers up and down the UK. It doesn't matter if you are not particularly proficient in a sport – clubs need people with bags of enthusiasm and commitment above anything else.

Family activities

If your children are reluctant to join a local club – maybe they feel nervous about being away from you or would prefer to do a more informal activity – there are lots of ways you can get active as a family without spending a fortune. Here are just a few ideas.

We usually think of walking and hiking as things we do in the countryside, but if you live in the middle of a city, that's no reason not to travel a short distance to go for a walk, or consider organizing an urban hike and take in the

Children's exercise preferences

Likes team sports – Football, rugby, cricket, netball

Likes sociable sports – Team sports, athletics

Likes competing – Tennis, football, athletics

Likes the outdoors – Hiking, skiing, cycling

Likes being coached – Swimming, gymnastics, horse riding, athletics, dance

Likes a pure physical challenge – Gym sessions, running, aerobics

Likes family activities – Hiking, skiing, cycling, swimming

Likes combative sports – Rugby, fencing, martial arts

Likes doing what other children do – Football, skateboarding, horse riding sights as you go. Make use of local sports grounds and parks – children love a game of five-a-side or a knockabout. Get friends and parents involved for a full game, but if you don't have enough people try playing penalties or kicking tries. Rounders, softball and French cricket are also perfect park games for a sunny day.

Children go absolutely mad for adventure playgrounds – so much so that it's worth travelling a good distance to find one. They're physical, but they also incorporate a variety of activities to keep children interested – as well as an element of exploration and creativity, such as thinking of imaginative ways to get from A to B. You can either join in or watch from a safe distance!

Swimming baths also offer low-cost, high-fun exercise for all the family. Children can either swim lengths or just mess about – both are brilliant workouts and will help your children become confident around water. You can also get other children to come along and make it even more sociable. Local pools offer swimming classes if your child needs tuition.

Prefers individual sports – Tennis, squash, athletics, watersports

Prefers solitary sports – Jogging, cycling, swimming

Plays more to enjoy it – Climbing, hiking, skiing, horse riding

Prefers the indoors – Swimming, ballet, squash

Prefers teaching themselves – Skateboarding

Enjoys a mental challenge too – Orienteering, dance

Prefers time away from the family – Skateboarding, ballet, gymnastics

Likes gentle sports – Ballet, dance, gymnastics, ice skating, horse riding, yoga

Likes doing something different from other children – Martial arts, gymnastics

Let your child choose

All children are different. It's obvious really, but it's amazing how much difference there can be (even between young children of the same sex) in terms of what they enjoy and what they don't. Some children revel in the outdoors, some couldn't think of anything worse; some children love being taught a new game or skill, and some just like being left to their own devices.

If your children are at the age when parents are just too embarrassing for words and they'd rather be seen dead than be seen exercising with mum and dad, there are lots of sports they can try by themselves. Your children will love the sense of independence it gives them and you can relax in the knowledge that they're getting fit and healthy in the process.

The table on pages 48–9 is designed to help you think about what your child might enjoy. Consider each of these preferences and how your child fits into them. Are they mad keen on water? Do they like inventing their own games? Don't forget there are loads of other activities that are not mentioned here; it's not a complete list. For example, there's a wide range of team sports they can try other than football, rugby, cricket and netball.

Knowing your child really helps here, but if you're not sure, don't worry. Instead, encourage them to try lots of different things, and see what they enjoy best. Every dad wants their son to play football for their country, but wouldn't we be just as proud if it turned out to be cycling or squash?

Try not to assume too much about what your child will like because of their sex, age or physical shape. We tend to assume that boys like football and girls like ballet – but that's not always true. If your daughter suddenly announces that she wants to give karate a go, why not? Correspondingly, if your son is quite small for his age, rugby might not seem like the ideal sport – but you never know.

Children – fads and fashion

Almost all children like the feeling of being cool and fashionable and therefore popular with their peers. This may be more important for some than others, but it's a pretty universal theme these days. Peer pressure will affect your children in all sorts of ways during their childhood (and later on, for that matter), and sometimes in unhealthy ways.

The good news is that, unlike other forms of peer pressure, when it comes to exercise, peer pressure is not entirely a bad thing. At the end of the day, you want your children to enjoy sport and exercise. So, if your child wants to do a certain activity because their friends are doing it, go for it! Let them give it a try – encourage them as you would for any other interest.

Children are no different when it comes to sports and activities. From a very early age, they learn that certain sports and activities have a 'cool' factor that others don't. Here are just a few common 'cool' examples:

- Skateboarding.
- Snowboarding.
- Rollerblading.
- Ice hockey.
- Martial arts (such as karate, tae kwon do).
- Horse riding.
- Ballet.

The last two on this list might not seem that cool, but they illustrate the point that the 'cool' factor can be an incentive for children to get involved in almost anything. If other children at school are doing it, they'll want to as well.

Kris's Top Tips

Be a role model

It's no use telling your children they should do more exercise if they see you slobbing in front of the TV every night. Your children will follow your example, so dust off those trainers and get active!

Be supportive

For children to participate in their chosen sport, they sometimes need a lot of input from their parents. This can translate as lifts to and from the sports venue, your presence as a spectator to cheer them along, or just flexibility in moving around mealtimes to accommodate games and practice sessions.

Have faith

You need to believe that your child can be good at sport – children are quick to pick up on any doubts you may have about their physical abilities. Let them work out for themselves what they can and can't do.

Love the outdoors

While rainy days can sometimes prevent you from playing sport, nothing should stop you from taking exercise outdoors. Children need fresh air and they also need to expand their horizons and be confident away from home. Wrap up warm and go splash in the puddles!

Limit the TV

While television has its uses on occasion, too much TV can prevent your child from getting physical exercise. It also encourages bad eating habits and weight gain. (See Chapter 1.)

Walk or cycle to school

If it's safe to do so, encourage your children to walk or cycle to school. If you are worried about your child travelling alone, why not encourage them to walk or cycle with a friend, or accompany them yourself?

Start them young

The younger you get your children into exercise and sport, the better. An active child is much more likely to be an active adult.

Play and have fun

Physical exercise doesn't have to mean competitive sport – children also need to be allowed simply to play. A knockabout in the park is just as beneficial as playing sport in a top league. Encourage them simply to have fun and enjoy themselves.

Get involved

Local clubs always need volunteers to help them coach or manage a team, so why not get involved? If you don't want to be a coach you could always help in other ways – by cheering loudly or making the half-time refreshments. This will allow you to enjoy an activity with your child and show them that you support what they're doing.

Don't push

Above all, children need to choose their own physical exercise or sport. As a parent the best thing you can do is to find out what your child is interested in and then offer gentle encouragement.

Peer pressure doesn't work only for the latest 'in thing', though – it can make a child want to play a really popular sport, such as football.

One problem that can crop up is cost. Very few parents can afford to indulge every whim of their child. Most children at some stage have demanded something for Christmas, such as a pair of rollerblades or a skateboard, which has then not been used after Boxing Day. If your child wants to try something new, be totally supportive – but if it involves significant cost up front, make it clear that they have to give it a proper go, and not just give up if they're bored after the first session. A sensible way to limit costs is to start off with second-hand equipment and then buy brand-new gear if they keep up the interest. Internet auction sites are great for finding second-hand sports equipment.

chapter 3

Sleep

Many children get less sleep than they need. In fact, in a recent study, children were asked about their sleep patterns and as many as half said they weren't getting enough and that they found it difficult to stay awake during the day. With all the other parental worries, does it really matter if your child isn't getting a good night's rest?

Why is sleep important?

The best way to understand why sleep is important for children is to understand what happens when they don't get enough of it. While the occasional poor night's rest won't do any long-term damage, sleep deprivation over time can have devastating consequences on schoolwork, behaviour and family life.

After a bad night's sleep you'll notice that the first thing to go is your ability to think clearly. Luckily, all you need is a good night's rest and you feel normal again. With chronic sleep loss, however, failing to get adequate rest night after night has a serious impact on your brain's ability to function properly. You feel groggy and forgetful, you find it more difficult to concentrate or make decisions, and your attention span shortens. In fact, research has shown that after just one night's missed sleep your brain feels as fuzzy as if you had drunk two glasses of wine. Imagine how confusing and disorientating that must be for a child. It's particularly difficult for them to monitor themselves and realize they are tired if that is how they always feel.

Sleep and schoolwork

If sleep deprivation impairs your attention, decision-making, communication and planning abilities, it's easy to see how children with sleep problems would find life at school difficult. Sleep-deprived children perform worse on most mental tasks – about a fifth of primary school children who have sleep problems also experience academic problems. Similarly, teenagers who don't get enough shut-eye are more likely to struggle or fail at school, all things being equal.

Lack of sleep even affects the higher mental faculties, such as abstract thinking and creativity. One recent study found that a good night's sleep helped volunteers crack a complicated number puzzle they couldn't solve the day before. It's as if 'sleeping on a problem' gives your brain a chance to restructure the information and come up with a new solution.

Sleep also helps our brain to store and organize information. The brain 'rescues' memories during the night that have been lost during the previous day. In other words, things you thought you had forgotten at the end of a long day are refreshed while you sleep. Sleep also helps some memories mature while discarding other, unimportant ones.

Conversely, a bit of extra sleep seems to improve a school child's performance. A study among Israeli primary school children found that as little as one hour extra of sleep had a marked effect on their grades. The children (aged between nine and 11) were tested before and after they had either an hour's extra sleep or an hour less. The children who had the extra hour performed significantly better on memory and attention-span tests compared with those who lost an hour's sleep. In fact, some of the children performed as well as children two years their senior. Reaction times were also better among the children who got an extra 60 minutes in bed.

The world record for the longest period of time a human being has gone without sleep is 264 hours, set by Randy Gardner in 1965. After 11 days awake the 17-year-old high-school student reported symptoms including slurred speech, mood swings, memory lapses, difficulty concentrating, paranoia and hallucinations.

Sleep and behaviour

As well as on school performance, lack of sleep can have a profound impact on a child's behaviour at home. Research has shown that young children who experience sleep problems are more likely to smoke, drink or use drugs as adults. Boys are also more susceptible than girls – those who have early childhood sleep problems are more than twice as likely to have started using alcohol by age 14, to smoke, and to use illicit drugs, compared with boys who don't have sleep problems. The reasons behind this are still unclear, but one theory is that children who have never learned to sleep properly are more likely to turn to alcohol and other drugs as adults to help them to relax and unwind.

Poor sleep patterns can leave children feeling tired and irritable, making it difficult for them to socialize with friends and family. They can also result in them feeling anxious and depressed. Children with persistent sleep problems tend to have poorer relationships with their parents and other children, whereas those who sleep well usually have higher self-esteem and are better able to control their aggression.

Children who are sleepy during the daytime are more likely to be clumsy and hurt themselves in an accident. An Italian study found that young boys who slept for less than ten hours a night had a greater chance of ending up in Accident and Emergency, and that this association was particularly strong among boys attending nursery school. Both boys and girls who go to bed late are also more likely to be involved in accidents in the home, the peak time for injury being between 4pm and midnight.

Any parent will tell you that a child who hasn't slept properly is more likely to be moody and find it difficult to control their impulses and anger. They also struggle to focus on one task and are more likely to be fidgety, inattentive and disruptive. There is increasing evidence that this type of behaviour is sometimes misdiagnosed by both parents and health professionals as attention deficit/hyperactivity disorder, when the real problem is simply lack of adequate sleep.

Sleep and health

Sleep deprivation doesn't just have a negative impact on learning and behaviour; it can also affect your child's physical health.

Poor sleep patterns may also be linked to obesity. Hormones that control appetite and weight gain are released during sleep and research has found that people who sleep on average only five hours a night have more of the hormones which make you feel hungry and less of those which make you feel full, compared with people who sleep for eight hours. The study concludes that this difference in hormone levels increases appetite and could lead to overeating.

If poor sleep is more likely to make you obese, the bad news is that obese children are more likely to suffer from sleep problems. The link between sleep apnoea (page 65) and obesity has been well documented. It's thought that 80 per cent of children who are classed as very obese also suffer from sleep apnoea. If their sleep is disrupted, an obese child is more likely to wake up feeling hungry. It's a vicious circle.

What's stopping my child from getting a good night's sleep?

A child might not sleep for a number of reasons. Some problems are medical, such as restless leg syndrome, while some are behavioural, such as stress or anxiety. One of the biggest barriers to good sleep, however, is lifestyle.

Hot topic How much sleep is enough?

This table shows the recommended average number of hours' sleep that a child needs per day, taking into account daytime naps. Note that from the age of four, which is also when they start school, children need to get all these requirements from the night-time sleep.

Age	Night-time sleep (hours)	Daytime sleep (hours)	Total sleep (hours)
1 month	8.5 (many naps)	7.5 (many naps)	16
3 months	6–10	5–9	15
6 months	10–12	3–4.5	14.5
9 months	11	3 (2 naps)	14
12 months	11	2.5 (2 naps)	13.5
18 months	11	2.5 (1–2 naps)	13.5
2 years	11	2 (1 nap)	13
3 years	10.5	1.5 (1 nap)	12
4 years	11.5	0	11.5
5 years	11	0	11
6 years	10.5–11	0	10.5–11
7 years	10.5	0	10.5
8 years	10–10.5	0	10–10.5
9 years	10	0	10
10 years	9.5–10	0	9.5–10
11 years	9.5	0	9.5
12–13 years	9–9.5	0	9–9.5
14 years	9	0	9
15 years	8.5–9	0	8.5–9
16 years	8.5	0	8.5

Lifestyle

A fifth of all young children get between two and five hours' less sleep than they need, every night. One of the main reasons seems to be that children stay up late to play computer games or watch TV in their bedroom and so become overstimulated by technology. They then find it difficult to unwind and get to sleep, instead of having a relaxing, calming bedtime routine. Mobile phones are also to blame, with children regularly spending the evening texting under the bed covers when they should be asleep.

Even if your child doesn't have a bedroom packed with technology, the television can still be a barrier to good sleep. Younger children who watch a lot of TV are more likely to display bedtime resistance, take longer to fall asleep and, on average, get less sleep than those who watch less TV. The reasons for this are not entirely clear, but the fact that children who watch lots of television tend to eat badly, weigh more, take less exercise and find it difficult to have 'quiet time' must be significant.

How much caffeine are children drinking?

Drink	Caffeine content
Filter coffee	200 mg
Instant coffee	140 mg
Red Bull	109 mg
Tea	100 mg
Iced tea	70 mg
Diet Coke	45 mg
Dr Pepper	41 mg
Pepsi	38 mg
Coca-Cola	34 mg
Hot chocolate/cocoa	10 mg
Chocolate milk	8 mg

Bedtime routine

Lots of young children refuse to go to bed or stay in their bedroom when it's time for sleep, while other children will go to bed, but only after a great deal of fuss. This is known as 'bedtime resistance' and is one of the most common and frustrating problems that parents face. As a result, many parents simply give up and let their children dictate their own bedtime or fall asleep in front of the TV. While this is an understandable, low-hassle approach for mum and dad, the reality is that having an inconsistent or non-existant bedtime routine actually makes the problem worse. Children who choose their own bedtime rarely go up at the right time, which means they end up going to bed too late, don't get enough sleep and feel pooped during the day.

Diet

Diet can also play a large part in either keeping children awake or helping them to relax. Caffeine, for example, interferes with a child's ability to sleep. It is a stimulant – it keeps us lively and active during the day but it can also stop

us from getting a good night's rest. The more caffeine a child has in their bloodstream at bedtime, the longer it will take them to fall asleep and the more disrupted their sleep will be.

We don't imagine that children drink products containing caffeine – after all, how many young children regularly drink tea or coffee? In reality, however, caffeine is present in lots of children's foods such as cola, chocolate, iced tea and coffee ice cream, as well as infant pain relievers and other over-the-counter medicines. Caffeinated energy drinks contain even more – a can of Red Bull, for example, contains three times the amount of caffeine as a can of Coke.

Healthy bedtime snacks

- One slice of wholemeal bread with a thin layer of smooth peanut butter.
- One banana.
- A handful of raisins.
- A small cup of sunflower seeds.
- A small bowl of plain porridge.
- One slice of wholemeal bread with a thin layer of yeast extract.
- One orange or clementine.
- A handful of blueberries or raspberries.
- A glass of skimmed milk – warm or cold.
- A cup of warm milk with a spoonful of honey stirred in.
- A cup of camomile, ginger, mint, lemon, peppermint or raspberry herbal tea.

Children have a smaller body than adults, so even a tiny amount of caffeine will have a bigger effect on them and does them no good. For an idea of the caffeine content of various drinks, see the table on pages 60–1.

Children who consume large amounts of fizzy drinks containing caffeine tend to take longer to get to sleep, are more likely to have broken sleep and get less sleep overall. They also tend to be sleepier during the day than children who consume less. The problem is that caffeine drinkers often drink more caffeine during the day to compensate for the fact they feel tired, but this lethargy is because caffeine is keeping them awake at night, and so the cycle continues.

Sugar is also responsible for disrupting sleep patterns in children. Consuming lots of sugary foods or fizzy drinks, especially in the evening, can cause wakefulness and irritability because your blood sugar levels crash in the middle of the night. The combination of caffeine and sugar found in many children's drinks, therefore, is a sure-fire recipe for a sleepless night.

Cigarettes

Smoking is bad for young people in numerous ways but one lesser-known side-effect is its ability to interfere with sleep. Children who smoke cigarettes are more likely to have problems getting to sleep and staying asleep and will have a poorer quality of sleep. This is because nicotine is a powerful stimulant, just like caffeine, and can lead to frequent and long-lasting sleep problems. You might think that smoking doesn't affect younger children, but research shows that as many as one in ten 11- to 15-year-olds is a regular smoker and that every day in Great Britain about 450 children start smoking.

Passive smoking also affects a child's ability to sleep. Inhaling second-hand cigarette smoke on a regular basis can lead to respiratory illnesses, such as asthma, which are a common cause of sleep problems.

Sleep disorders

Even if your children have a great bedtime routine, eat well and don't keep themselves awake with stimulants, they may still suffer from sleep deprivation as a result of a medical condition. At present 25 per cent of the UK population suffer from this type of sleep disorder.

Snoring

We don't snore when we are awake because the muscles in our mouth, nose and upper throat can keep the airway open. However, when we sleep, these muscles relax. If the muscles go really floppy, they partially block the airway and vibrate when we breathe in and out – this is snoring. If we have a cold or a blocked nose, the sound of these vibrations is amplified even more. Snoring is often seen as an old man's condition, but it's surprisingly common in children. There is a number of reasons why a child can snore:

■ Obesity – this is because being overweight can lead to an increase in fat around the throat and reduced muscle tone. The airways may also be narrowed and more likely to vibrate.

■ Infected tonsils or adenoids.

■ Smoking cigarettes – smoke irritates and blocks the nasal area, making it difficult to breathe at night. Even children who passively smoke have a greater risk of snoring; children with parents who smoke are more likely to snore than children of non-smoking parents.

■ Nasal irritation caused by dust and pet allergies. Asthma can also be a cause.

■ Occasionally a child's jaw shape can cause them to snore, but this problem usually resolves itself as the child grows.

We all know that snoring is annoying if you have to listen to it, but is it such a big deal if your child snores? Are they even affected by their own snoring? Well, research has shown that snoring does more than just get on the rest of the family's nerves. In a study of over 1000 children it was revealed that those who snored (which was about 10 per cent) were more likely to get bad marks at school, especially in maths and English. This is because snorers breathe in less oxygen while they're asleep, which prevents them from getting a good night's sleep and has the knock-on effect of making it more difficult for them to concentrate at school the next day.

Children whose parents snore can also be adversely affected. If an adult member of the family has a particularly loud or persistent snoring problem, it can prevent the rest of the house from getting a good night's sleep.

Sleep apnoea

An extreme version of snoring is called 'sleep apnoea'. The word apnoea comes from the Greek *apnea*, which means 'want of breath' – in fact the sufferer stops breathing in their sleep and wakes up gasping for breath.

Sleep apnoea is caused by the same muscles that affect snoring – it happens when the muscles at the back of the throat and the soft palate relax to the point of blocking the airway. When this happens the sufferer can stop breathing for up to 25 seconds; the brain, which is starved of oxygen, sends an

emergency signal and makes the sufferer gasp or snort for air. In a single night, a person with sleep apnoea can be woken in this way up to 350 times, which inevitably leads to tiredness the next day. Sleep apnoea has also been linked to an increased risk of stroke, heart attack and high blood pressure.

Obese children are the most likely youngsters to suffer from sleep apnoea, but for much of the time it goes undiagnosed. In a recent study of obese children, more than 85 per cent were suffering from some form of sleep apnoea, with a quarter of these suffering the most severe form of the condition. Left untreated, children with sleep apnoea may suffer daytime sleepiness resulting in poor concentration and leading to poor performance at school.

Insomnia

Insomnia is a trickier condition to pin down. The term is used to describe a number of sleep problems including a prolonged inability to get a good night's

It's bedtime!

Age	Suggested bedtime (based on 7am wake-up)
Younger than 4 years	7.30pm (supplemented with naps during the day – see the table on page 59 for recommended amounts of sleep)
4 years	7.30pm
5–6 years	8pm
7–8 years	8–8.30pm
9–10 years	9–9.30pm
11–14 years*	9.30–10 pm
14–16 years*	No later than 10.30pm

*With older children it's often better not to be too rigid about bedtime: negotiate an approximate bedtime (e.g. between 9.30 and 10pm) to leave the child with some room for personal choice and manoeuvre. This will reduce the amount of bedtime conflict, but once you have made the agreement you need to try and stick to it.

sleep, trouble falling asleep, or waking up on a regular basis feeling unrefreshed and tired. About a third of the UK population, including children, suffers from insomnia and its effects include daytime tiredness, irritability and low moods.

It's difficult to establish the exact cause of insomnia in children, but stress and anxiety are thought to be major factors. Children who have had a recent traumatic life event, such as losing a parent or going through a family break-up, often suffer. Worries about exams, relationships and health can also severely interrupt sleep patterns. Caffeine, nicotine and high-sugar foods can also exacerbate the problem.

Restless leg syndrome

The fourth of the most common medical reasons why people fail to sleep is called restless leg syndrome (RLS). About one in 20 people suffers from this condition which causes a tingling, itching sensation or aches and pains in the legs. The sufferer has a poor night's rest because they have to keep moving their lower limbs around to relieve the discomfort.

While RLS is more common among older people, the condition can also affect children. Doctors often misdiagnose RLS in infants, mistaking it for growing pains or attention deficit disorder. Children with parents who have RLS are more likely to develop the condition than those without.

Solving sleep problems

If your child is suffering from a sleep problem, it can be difficult to establish whether the problem lies in their diet and lifestyle or whether the condition has a medical basis. While your GP should always be your first port of call if you are worried, it might be worth thinking about whether anything at home could be causing or contributing to the problem. Often a change in bedtime routine or a reduction in certain foods can be really beneficial. Most important, when you decide on a bedtime routine, stick to it! Therein lies the success of 'routines'. If you're not sure what time your child should be hitting the hay, follow the handy guide on page 66 to help you set a bedtime that is appropriate for the age of your child.

Kris's Top Tips

Make bedtime the same time every night

Believe it or or not, children love routines. They have very little control over their life, so predictability and consistency in the day can make them feel safe and secure. One of the best ways to ensure your child gets enough sleep is to set a firm and consistent bedtime. Routinely letting your child stay up late won't do them any favours, although it won't do any harm as the occasional treat, especially at weekends or during school holidays.

Create an enjoyable bedtime routine

Create a lovely, relaxing, 30-minute bedtime routine for your child. It will help them wind down and ease the transition between the noise and excitement of downstairs and the quiet darkness of the bedroom. It could include:

- A glass of warm milk before they brush their teeth.
- A healthy bedtime snack.
- A relaxing bath.
- A bedtime story or lullaby.
- A gentle conversation about the day.

Keep it exactly the same every evening, so the child looks forward to the predictability of the routine.

Take the TV out of the bedroom

Remove the TV, DVD and computer from your child's room – bedrooms are for sleeping. Older children may find this very difficult, so you might have to negotiate rules about using them instead – for instance, no playing computer games after a certain time.

Make sure the bedroom is comfortable

Children will sleep best in a cool, dark, quiet room. The ideal temperature is 16–18°C (60–65°F). You also need to make sure that noise from the rest of the house isn't disturbing them and that the room has adequate curtains or blinds – streetlights and sunrise can prevent a child from sleeping or can wake them up too early.

Invest in a good bed

Children often get the short straw when it comes to mattresses and beds, as they tend to get hand-me-downs from older members of the family or have the cheapest bed. Don't scrimp – a good-quality mattress is vital for sleep, so invest in the best you can afford for your child and make sure, too, that you use comfortable bedding such as pure cotton sheets (artificial fibres tend to make sheets too hot).

Watch what and when they eat

A good diet and a healthy weight are key to good sleep. (See Chapter 1 for advice on a balanced diet for your family.) Don't let your children eat too late – eating a large, heavy meal late at night, especially if it's spicy or fatty, will interfere with their sleep. Watch the caffeine and refined sugar intake too – absolutely no caffeine or fizzy drinks after 4pm.

Tire them out

One of the best ways to ensure that children enjoy a good night's sleep is to encourage them to get enough physical activity during the day. Just be careful not to let them exercise too close to bedtime as it produces stimulants that may keep them awake for a while.

Talk to your child

It might sound obvious, but try asking your child if there is anything that is bothering them – worries about exams, bullying, school, family life or friendships can cause children a lot of anxiety and lead to insomnia. (Chapter 10 will help you to communicate with your child in a loving and stress-free way.)

Look into alternative remedies

Aromatherapy can be very relaxing. The essential oils used in aromatherapy act on the nervous system and can have a calming effect. Not all essential oils are suitable for children, however, but both lavender and camomile are safe to use. Essential oils are very strong, so follow the manufacturer's instructions and never use them undiluted on the skin.

See your GP

If you've tried everything and the problem still continues, see your GP. There could be an underlying sleep disorder or sleep-disrupting allergy that needs identifying. The good news is that most sleep disorders in children can be sorted out.

chapter 4

Learning

Children are constantly learning and there is so much more to it than simply what happens at school. A child's attitude to learning is strongly influenced by that of their parents. Research shows that the amount of involvement parents have in their child's learning and education will affect their academic performance – so encourage them to enjoy it.

Do we need a good education?

Although it's not the only thing that brings us happiness and success, a good education gives us a real advantage in life, in more ways than one. It's amazing the number of people who say that they wish they had worked harder at school. As children, we simply don't realize what an important part education will play in the rest of our life. By the time we're adults, however, we have come to understand this link.

How we view learning

The general attitude to education has changed massively in the last 40 years, at every level and in every age group. Here's a quick example – in 1960 just one in 20 children went to university; today, that figure is one in three.

One of the biggest changes is the greater focus on the basics, such as reading, writing and mathematics. In itself this is certainly a good thing, because it has ensured that higher numbers of children are leaving school armed with the skills that they need in order to progress in the workplace and life in general.

But these developments have also come at a cost: focusing on basic skills may mean a reduction in the number of subjects that children study at primary and secondary level. This in turn places a greater burden on parents to provide additional teaching and to encourage a wider range of interests to help shape their children into 'rounded' adults.

How children learn

When children start school it can be quite a relief for many parents, who suddenly find themselves with more time on their hands. Unfortunately, it's also quite tempting to think that the school will simply take over your child's education and that you can just deal with the home stuff. But if you really want to help the progress of your child's learning, you need to spend time with them before they are old enough to go to school as well as once they've started.

The first thing to do is understand the principles of learning – which effectively means knowing how young minds work – and then to learn how to help your children to keep exercising those principles.

Concentration and attention span

Before we start, let's define these terms: concentration is the ability to focus on a single activity, or event, at the exclusion of everything else; whereas attention span is the length of time that we can maintain a basic level of concentration. These are both important skills for a child to learn.

So why is it that there is so much variation in how well children can concentrate, and how good their attention span is? The answer to this question lies in the human brain. Technically, it is an organ, but in many ways it is easier to think of it as a muscle. For basic health it needs regular exercise, just as our other muscles do, and by training the brain carefully you can increase its abilities in many areas – memory, concentration, attention span, flexibility and imagination, to name just a few. As with physical exercise, we never know what our brain is really capable of unless it is carefully and safely stretched. And, as

is the case with our body, many mental abilities can deteriorate or be lost completely if we neglect our brain.

Admittedly, there is a degree of genetic variation in terms of what we are physically capable of, and this is also true of our mental abilities. But whatever children are born with, it's what they choose to do with their abilities that really counts – such as how well they keep their brain healthy, the extent to which they exercise it, and how much they try to explore and stretch it to its full potential.

A lifelong love of learning

In general children, and many adults too, tend to view education and learning as a chore. It is crucial that parents avoid this attitude: very few children enjoy all of their lessons at school, but there's no reason why they shouldn't enjoy most of them. And this is where you come in.

Encourage your children to enjoy learning from the very first opportunity. This pleasure comes from the earliest days, and even in infancy we are teaching our children constantly – about food, about their environment, about discipline and about play. The sooner you steer them towards enjoying learning, the better.

■ Encourage and guide learning at home. Make sure that your child does at least one thing a week that involves mastering something they don't study at

school – it could be a musical instrument, a puzzle, or just an interest in something like cars or animals.

- ■ Reward effort in both schoolwork and learning at home.
- ■ Be enthusiastic about all of your children's learning.
- ■ Explain to your children at every stage why something is worth learning. As adults we tend to be happier working at something when we know there is a reason for doing so, and children are usually the same.

Parents as role models

We've seen in previous chapters how children often take their lead from their parents in all sorts of things – such as diet, exercise and sleep – but the same is also true of learning.

There are lots of ways in which you can act as an educational role model for your child. Here are just a few:

If you did well at school

Tell them how much you enjoyed school and learning new things and your enthusiasm will rub off on them. BUT – and this is a big but – be careful not to put too much pressure on them.

Take a course or learn a new skill

When was the last time you learnt something new? Perhaps you'd like to do a basic course in a language, or learn to play a musical instrument? Perhaps there's something you've always wanted to do, like ride a horse or know how a car engine works? It's not too late, so take a home-learning course, or perhaps an evening course, and show your children that learning is always valuable and worthwhile.

'I haven't been to school for nearly 20 years – how can I be a good example to my children when it comes to education?'

Take an interest in what your children learn

Talk to your children at least once a week about what they've been learning in school. This might seem an obvious thing to do, and sometimes children might be reluctant to tell you, so try simply saying, 'Tell me something I don't know' (meant honestly, of course...). If you've ever watched a child playing with a younger sibling or friend, you'll notice that they enjoy teaching and explaining things as much as they do learning, but they don't get the chance to do it very often. This interaction is also a great opportunity for children to feel that their relationship with their parents works both ways.

Different learning styles suit different children

Time for a little psychology. There is a well-established theory that says that almost all of us respond best to one of three styles of learning. The evidence seems to be that whichever category we fall into is innate – we're like that from birth – and so this model also applies to children:

Visual learning (through what is seen)

- This style appears to be the one that most people respond to, as around 65 per cent of the population, or two in three people, learn this way.
- This approach teaches using written information, notes, diagrams and pictures.
- A person who learns best this way will also learn well using TV programmes and videos.

Auditory learning (through what is heard)

- Most successful for around 30 per cent of the population, or one in three people.
- People responding to this method learn best through what they hear, particularly by talking and listening.
- Someone who learns in an auditory way will like both quiet study and lively discussions.

Kinaesthetic learning (through touch, movement and space)

- This is quite a rare response – only around 5 per cent of the population or one in 20 people prefer to learn this way. As the smallest group, it can often be disadvantaged by formal education.

It seems obvious, but it's amazing how often it's missed: two of the most common causes of learning difficulties in young children are problems with vision and hearing, and very often neither of these is diagnosed for months or even years into a child's education. Bear in mind, too, that many children don't know what their eyes and ears ought to be capable of; or, if they are aware that they have a problem with seeing or hearing, they might be too embarrassed to tell anyone about it.

■ These people learn best through physical activity, imitation and practice.
■ A common trait of someone who learns this way is to enjoy tinkering with things (both objects and concepts), in order to understand them better.

What all this means is that your child will probably respond best to learning information that is presented in one of these three styles. You don't have to be a child psychologist to analyze this: simply watch them carefully over the years as they develop their learning style, and before long it should be fairly clear which approach suits them. Once you know this, you can support your child's learning by helping them to learn in the way that is most helpful to them.

If your child is struggling with learning, either at home or in the classroom, having their eyes and ears tested should be one of your first ports of call (if this hasn't already been seen to within the last six months).

Reading

Most children learn to read at some point between the ages of four and seven. Just as with all sorts of other skills, the time of arrival at this developmental milestone varies greatly, and this is not necessarily indicative of their intelligence. If your child seems to be taking longer to learn to read than their friends or classmates, don't panic, and don't assume that this is going to be the pattern for the rest of their education.

If you are keen to get your child reading, there are loads of things you can do to help them, both before they start school and during the early school years. Interest in language starts literally from birth – babies love being talked, sung and read to. Repetition is also helpful, and babies and small children love the familiarity of hearing the same story, poem or song over and over again.

Remember, too, that words don't just belong in books. Words are everywhere – on TV, posters, signposts and in shops, to name just a few places. From the earliest possible opportunity, encourage any interest your child shows in words – both while they're in the home and out and about.

Get them riveted by reading

The Department for Education has given out some great tips on encouraging early interest in words and reading:

- Play I-Spy – an excellent game to demonstrate to children that certain words begin with certain letters.

- At the shops, point out the different names of foods as you go past them – even if the word isn't written on a label.

- Let your child choose their favourite book and read it to them as often as possible. Apart from helping them with language, reading to children can also be a great way of getting them to sleep.

- Early on, show your child that words go from left to right on a page and then down to the next line, by following the words with a finger as you read them.

- Don't keep children guessing for too long about how to say a word – say it slowly, pronouncing each set of letters one at a time, before gradually saying it more quickly.

- Don't be afraid to let your children develop their own reading style – slow and careful, or faster and not worrying about mistakes. Children read differently, just as adults do.

How schools teach reading

There are, in fact, three separate methods by which children are taught to read at school. In the past, individual teachers and schools tended to focus on just one of these methods, but over time it became apparent that a combination of the three was the most effective strategy. Check with your child's teacher which method they are using – it can be very disruptive if you start to teach your child at home using a different method.

These are the three methods by which reading is most commonly taught. (Note that the 'At home' sections are exercises that you can help your child with as soon as they are ready – typically from age two upwards.)

1 Look and say

This is the simplest of the three methods. The child is encouraged to learn whole words without breaking them down into syllables or groups of consonants. The core skill is 'whole word recognition' – meaning that the child memorizes the shape of the word – and it works well early on for important words. One problem with this method is that it doesn't teach the child any patterns that can be applied to new words, which means that every word must be learnt individually.

At home: Make small paper labels with the name of an object on them, and stick them to that object – such as 'chair' or 'table'. For really important words, like your child's name, write it on a card, mix it with other words on cards, and get your child to pick out their name.

2 Phonics

Phonics teaches children sounds that are made by syllables and clusters of letters, as well as the rules underlying these sounds. First, the child is taught a very simple word like 'cat', then other words are introduced with the same sounds – like 'hat', 'rat', and 'mat'. The idea is that by repeating words with

Dyslexia

The word 'dyslexia' comes from the Greek language and means 'difficulty with words'. For all the myths that surround it, that really is the simplest way to describe the condition. Dyslexia is caused by a difference (as opposed to a defect) in the area of the brain that deals with language, which affects the basic mental skills needed for learning to read, write and spell. Psychologists have shown that dyslexic people process information differently from non-dyslexics.

Though dyslexia is very common, as with ADHD (see pages 82–3) there is not a crystal-clear boundary between those with the condition and those without it – it's less 'black and white' and more 'shades of grey'. But the British Dyslexia Association believes that around 4 per cent of the population is severely dyslexic and a further 6 per cent have mild to moderate problems with words.

Dyslexia occurs in people from all backgrounds and of all abilities; from people who cannot read to those with university degrees. It can emerge or be diagnosed at any point during a child's education and, increasingly often, in adulthood. The most common signs of dyslexia are:

- Difficulty with reading, despite average or high intelligence in other areas.
- Difficulty with sequences, such as problems with getting dates in order.
- Erratic spelling.
- Poor organization and lack of time management.
- Difficulty organizing thoughts clearly.

Dyslexic people of all ages can learn effectively, but they may need to be taught using different approaches. The condition is no reflection of the IQ of the child, or of their performance in school.

Dyslexia is a puzzling mix of both difficulties and strengths. Dyslexic people often have distinctive talents that non-dyslexics don't have, like excellent the same sounds and groups of letters, children can apply the rule they have learnt to new words with the same group of letters as and when they encounter them. Phonics are very effective for most children, but are particularly successful with dyslexic or slower-reading children, who tend to rely on sounds to learn to read.

At home: Say single-letter sounds (for example, 't t t t t') and get your child to repeat them. Also, try playing basic games of I-Spy – but only with uncomplicated words that have a simple first consonant.

3 Whole language

This method is the one that relies most on the child's ability to improvise. Children are taught whole language by being given simple texts or books to read, based on previous experiences of language which are often picked up using 'Look and say' and 'Phonics'. This approach requires the child to have the confidence to try a word, and sometimes even guess it. Pictures are often used and through them the child is taught to 'read' the story. Although difficult, it's perhaps the best way to encourage more advanced readers.

At home: Read a favourite book to your child and try getting them to finish a phrase that they know well, such as 'Once upon a...'. Encourage your child to learn nursery rhymes and simple poems off by heart.

problem-solving and creativity, as well as some or all of the usual difficulties. Dyslexics who have been very successful in later life include Agatha Christie, Albert Einstein, Richard Branson, Felicity Kendall, Steven Redgrave, Benjamin Zephaniah and Robbie Williams.

Having a label doesn't actually make that much difference to the child – it's just that they are going to need a little extra help.

Finally, the same also applies to dyslexia as with ADHD with regard to labelling. If your child is diagnosed with dyslexia, it's really important not to get too fixated with the label. Your child is still normal, with his or her own unique talents and personality, like any other child. With your help, they can adapt to the condition and still fulfil all their potential to become successful, happy adults.

For more information, see Further resources.

Hot topic ADHD

What is ADHD?

If you have school-age children, it's likely that you've heard of a condition known as ADHD. It stands for attention deficit/hyperactivity disorder. Although it affects both children and adults, nowadays it is usually diagnosed in childhood. It is characterized by poor concentration, impulsiveness, overactivity (higher-than-normal energy and activity levels), distractibility and a lack of inhibition with people they don't know. At school the child seems unable to sit still and stay quiet for more than a few moments, and as a result they often disturb others. But ADHD isn't a disease or illness like measles – there is no simple, black-and-white boundary between those who have it and those who don't.

There is evidence that ADHD is at least partially genetic, but it has also been associated with difficulties in upbringing, including a lack of clear boundaries, or a lack of attention from parents. A combination of genetic factors and difficulties in upbringing can often lead to a diagnosis of ADHD; however, some children have such a genetic vulnerability that they would develop ADHD even with 'perfect' parenting.

Although there is broad agreement that ADHD is a real condition, experts disagree on how many children are actually affected by it. Current estimates are anywhere between one in 20 and one in 50 children, and boys are three times more likely than girls to be diagnosed.

ADHD can affect language development and learning to read. The learning difficulties resulting from ADHD can be challenging enough, but the other reason why ADHD is a concern for both parents and educationalists is that it can contribute to a wide range of other behavioural and social problems. Children with ADHD often suffer emotional difficulties because they aren't like their peers, and their school marks tend to be lower than average. It can be very frustrating not to be able to do something their classmates take for granted, such as reading a page in a book.

The good news is that many children with ADHD go on to do well in later life. It's possible that it is the nature of schooling alone that ADHD children struggle with, as opposed to the much greater variety of skills required in life outside school.

How to detect it

Diagnosing ADHD is a complicated and skilled process and all symptoms should be assessed by experienced child psychologists before a judgement is made. Even if you think you recognize some of the tell-tale signs in your child, it doesn't necessarily mean they have ADHD.

When children are getting lower academic results than their intelligence suggests they should be achieving, some parents look to ADHD as an explanation for a problem that might actually be caused by other factors, such as boredom or emotional difficulties. A wrong diagnosis of ADHD can seriously harm a child's development, particularly when the real answers may be closer to home.

How can parents help?

There's a great deal that parents themselves can do to reduce the problems associated with ADHD, but in a minority of cases professional help is also needed. Behavioural treatment is usually the first port of call and parents will be advised on how to make changes to the way that they care for their children in the home environment – including their approach to sleep, diet, exercise and interaction with their children. In rare cases drugs, including Ritalin, can be offered by a psychiatrist or paediatrician.

Whether or not you use drugs is entirely your decision. There is strong evidence that Ritalin and other drugs improve the concentration of children with ADHD, but most psychologists agree that they should be used as a last resort. There can also be side effects – these are rarely serious, but they are unpleasant enough to ensure that these drugs are not handed out in minor cases.

Living with ADHD

Finally, if your child is diagnosed with ADHD, it's vital that you don't become concerned with the label and let it change how you feel about them. They are still talented and unique, and with your help your child can adapt to the condition, often overcoming it completely, and live a normal and successful life. There are many celebrities with ADHD whose condition has not hampered their ambitions; these include Daniel Bedingfield, Tom Cruise, Jim Carrey, Billy Connolly and Whoopi Goldberg.

For more information, see Further resources.

In the last 20 years, psychologists have identified a condition that is similar to dyslexia, but the problem occurs with numbers, rather than words. It's the rather awkwardly named dyscalculia. Children with dyscalculia show many of the equivalent symptoms to dyslexia, such as getting numbers the wrong way round, but they might also have more trouble with mental and written arithmetic than would be expected for their intelligence. If this seems the case with your child, it might be worth talking to a specialist to develop strategies for helping your child with their maths. Later in life dyscalculia shows up in poor timekeeping and an inability to keep track of money. To find out more, see Further resources.

Qualifications

There is far more to a good education than just gaining a set of qualifications. When it comes to jobs and careers, there's an unfortunate truth about qualifications: they tend to be forgotten almost as soon as you start your first real job. Nine out of ten employers will tell you that they consider work experience to be far more important than academic qualifications.

But, rightly or wrongly, qualifications still play a very important part in determining career prospects because they make one really major difference – they help you get the job in the first place. The majority of employers will say that, although qualifications don't count for very much once you're in, they are used as a sort of filter for determining whom the employer might be interested in taking on, and whom they aren't.

One of the most important things for parents to bear in mind when it comes to qualifications is that they truly aren't the be-all and end-all. Whatever you were expecting, if your child gets lower grades than they were hoping for, you must keep calm. Your children will always look to you for a reaction to their achievements, and if you start to panic and think your child will never get a job or get into university, this will rub off on them. You need to coax your children gently into thinking optimistically and confidently about their future, even if there are setbacks along the way.

Girls and boys

The academic performance of girls at school has increased enormously over the last 20 years, and much more so than the performance of boys. A study in the US of 900 primary school children in 2002 revealed trends that have also been observed in the UK:

■ Girls performed better in school subjects including English, maths and humanities, whereas boys achieved higher results in science.

■ Girls worried more than boys about how well they did in school.

■ Boys were less concerned about academic performance than girls, particularly if they failed, so tended not to be disappointed by bad results.

There are all sorts of theories as to why girls are now doing so much better in school. Some people believe that girls are inherently better suited to classroom learning than boys, while others think that in mixed schools, girls are more able to concentrate in the presence of the opposite sex than boys. But one factor that has almost certainly been important is the greater aspirations that girls now harbour for having a career, and that both parents and teachers also have for them. Today the opportunities are there for girls at all stages of the education system in this country.

Homework

Unsurprisingly, research into the homework habits of children at secondary school confirms what we would expect – that for children over the age of 11, those who do their homework regularly perform better academically. But, interestingly, there is no consistent evidence that homework improves the performance of primary school children.

So why should really young children be made to do homework? In the view of the current government there's one overriding reason – that at that early stage homework strengthens the link between what happens at school and what happens at home and thereby encourages active involvement by the parents in their children's education.

But if homework can be such a chore, why do children have to do it anyway? Why isn't there a nice, simple divide between home and school life? Couldn't children just stay on after school to do their extra work, and then come home and relax? These questions seem fair enough, but there is one excellent reason why children are asked to do homework at home: it's about teaching them to take responsibility for their own learning. If children study only when they have a teacher breathing down their neck, they don't learn to motivate and discipline themselves to work independently.

A child's reluctance to do homework is very common and so, once again, you have an important part to play in how your child thinks about homework. With the right help from you, homework can become a simple, straightforward part of a child's daily life – and even something they enjoy doing. Three factors really help to make this happen – routine, environment and support.

Routine

It's exactly that – ensuring that your children knuckle down to their homework at a similar time each day, and early enough that they don't get tired halfway through. The best time for this tends to be early evening. Let your children have a nice break of an hour or so after school, then settle them down for homework. Try to make sure there is a set routine for homework at the weekend too. Very often homework is left until Sunday night, but most children enjoy their weekends more if they get it out of the way on Saturday and don't have it hanging over them.

Environment

This simply means the place and the conditions under which homework gets done. There are a few basic principles that should be observed as closely as possible:

■ First, they should do their homework in a room that is pleasant to be in: quiet, well lit and with as few distractions as possible. Children's bedrooms are not usually the best idea, as they tend to be full of toys and posters, so getting them to work in a dining room or a study is a better option.

■ Second, TV and music should not be allowed under any circumstances while homework is going on. Children will protest until the cows come home that they can work with music in the background – but all of the scientific evidence suggests that, with the exception of quiet classical music, this isn't the case.

■ Finally, friends and siblings doing homework together can actually improve their work, but this needs careful monitoring. Children can really motivate each other to get on with it and share ideas, but don't leave them alone to work in a room where they can chat and distract each other, unless you're certain they can be trusted to concentrate.

Support

This is where you can really make a difference. As I said before, research shows clearly that the amount of involvement parents have in their child's education strongly predicts their later academic performance. So:

The recommended guidelines for the amount of time children in the UK should spend on homework are:
Age 5–6: 1 hour a week
Age 7–8: 1–1.5 hours a week
Age 9–10: 30 minutes a day
Age 11–12: 45–90 minutes a day
Age 13–15: 1–2 hours a day
These figures are more than for some countries, but lower than for others. In the UK, homework tends to start earlier in life than for children of other countries, but older UK children seem to do less than in other countries.

■ Guide them, but don't do the work for them – if your child asks for your help, you'll have to strike a careful balance. On the one hand, answer any questions that will help their broad understanding of a subject if you can, but on the other, don't give them the complete answer to any question that they've been set – they might get a good mark, but they won't know why. Both you and their teachers need to have a clear picture of how well they understand what they're being taught and this picture will become blurred if you are effectively doing their work for them, even though it might be tempting to help them out at times.

■ In longer assignments that involve research, help your child in any way possible to get access to the sources they need. Take them to a library, show them useful sites on the internet and invest in books for them if it will help.

■ Take any opportunity you can to praise both high achievement and real effort. If your child is performing well in a subject, that's something to be encouraged, but it's equally important to commend perseverance with a subject or task that your child finds difficult. Make sure you reward effort rather than natural talent: if your child finds a particular subject very easy, don't reward them for a mark or exam result unless they've genuinely worked hard to achieve it.

■ Just as with work during school time, children need to understand the relevance of a piece of work to their own life: they need to know how the task relates to the rest of their learning, and why the work is valuable for them in the future.

■ Keep homework in perspective: it's valuable, but there is more to your child's learning and development than just sitting at a desk for hours on end, poring over textbooks.

Computers

Computers make invaluable homework aids in many ways, but these are two of the most important:

■ The internet contains a vast amount of information that can help with homework. There's lots of material available from trustworthy sources such as the Department for Education and the BBC, but also enormous amounts of information on particular subjects that can be found by using search engines. This way of learning encourages children to follow their particular curiosities about a subject, rather than stick to what is in the school textbook.

If you are concerned about harmful internet content, there are numerous programmes available that enable you to restrict what your children can access to certain sites. Start at www.thinkuknow.co.uk for more details.

■ Word-processing – this is a basic package for writing text that comes with most computers, such as Microsoft Word or WordPerfect. Once a child becomes a proficient typist, they'll find that they can do homework much more quickly on a computer than they can with pen and paper. The other really big advantage with word-processing for homework is that it is easier for children (and adults!) to edit, change, rewrite and experiment with their work before they hand it in at school. This encourages them to think through what they are communicating, and how they communicate it.

Kris's Top Tips

- Get involved with your children's schooling.
- Encourage them to LOVE learning.
- Remember that academic results, while important, are not the be-all and end-all of your child's education.
- Help them to get their homework done by creating routine and the right environment.
- Lead by example and learn something new yourself.
- Have their eyes and ears tested every two years.

- Show your children how to use the computer safely. If you don't have one, consider buying one.
- Help their reading as much as possible – but be patient.
- Be aware of learning differences, including dyslexia and ADHD, but don't allow them to influence how you think about your child and their future.
- Children learn best in different ways. Present them with books and information in different styles, and play to their strengths.

chapter 5

Love and praise

Can you love your children too much? Previous generations believed withholding affection strengthened a child's character, preparing him or her for the realities of life. Today we know the opposite to be true: the more love you show your children, the better adjusted they become. However, it is how you show love that makes the difference.

Can you spoil your children with love?

One of the main justifications behind the old way of parenting was that children are spoiled by too much love and affection. The 'school of hard knocks' approach believes that children need toughening up for the outside world and that too much parental affection in their formative years will make them weak and vulnerable adults. In particular, fathers were encouraged to behave coolly towards their sons for fear that any displays of affection towards them would make them 'feminine' and needy. Sadly, this belief is still held by a surprising number of parents. In fact, numerous studies have shown that male children still receive less physical affection than female children, even when they are babies.

So let's get one thing straight right now: this old-school type of parenting isn't good for children or parents. Detailed research by psychologists has shown that withholding affection from your children does not create well-adjusted people. The reality seems to be that the most emotionally challenged and needy adults are those who feel that they weren't shown enough love by their parents, whereas children who grow up being loved and cherished by their parents tend to become more emotionally healthy adults.

Forget the myth: it is simply not possible to spoil a child by showing them too much love. Problems arise only when you give a child 'things' instead of giving them love. Over-indulgent parents who buy their children endless toys and games, or who are lax about boundaries and routines, often

behave in this way to assuage their own feelings of guilt about not spending enough time with them. This is usually because they are attempting to hide other problems in the home – such as a marital break-up – but children are canny creatures, and even very young children know when gifts are being used as a substitute for real love and affection.

What do children want?

Most research into family relationships has looked at parenting from the mum and dads' perspective, and rarely have studies asked children how they feel about love and what matters to them.

In the BBC series *Child of Our Time*, over a thousand children were asked what they most wanted from their parents. Rather than the answers that you might expect – such as 'I want lots of toys' or 'I'd like a big house' – the overwhelming majority of children wanted the same thing. Across all age ranges, 'being there for me' and being trusted came top of the list, as did the importance of 'comfort and hugs' and 'talking with me'. While there were, inevitably, a few subtle differences between age groups and sexes (older children worried about financial security more than young children, for example), all the children in the study shared a wish for parents to be emotionally close and involved with them. This is what parental love is all about.

What happens when you withhold love?

At its most extreme, withholding love from your children can have a devastating effect. Children who experience a lack of love during their early years can go on to suffer a wide variety of problems in later life; and research has demonstrated that neglected children often become society's most dysfunctional adults. A lack of love, manifested in mistreatment or even just a parent's indifference to a child, has been implicated in some of our biggest social problems – from criminal behaviour in teenagers to sexual crimes. Any harsh, unloving parenting is often repeated in subsequent generations and unloved children often go on to be unloving parents, never having being shown how to express or receive love themselves.

Experts in youth crime prevention know that cold or rejecting parents are more likely to have children who commit crimes and lack normal inhibitions against offending. Indeed, an American study found that over 50 per cent of juvenile offenders had been neglected as children. Time and time again, studies show that troubled individuals, such as adolescent runaways, violent criminals and sexual offenders, often report childhood histories of physical, emotional or sexual abuse.

Thankfully, this type of unhappy scenario is not the norm and most parents feel very warmly towards their children. However, some parents could perhaps do more to demonstrate their love through their everyday behaviour. Common mistakes that many parents make – even when they dearly love their children – include persistent criticism, emotional withdrawal, not accepting children for who they are and forgetting to praise good behaviour. While these sorts of problems aren't in the same league as serious child abuse, undermining a child's confidence or failing to show them adequate affection can have long-term consequences.

What do children need?

For a child to thrive and develop into a happy, successful person, they need to feel safe, loved and accepted. Children need to be raised lovingly and non-violently and need to experience discipline that will motivate them through love, not fear. This does not mean giving in to them all the time; showing love can be about boundaries. Children from these types of homes can be remarkably resilient and can weather many storms. A child who feels unloved and insecure, on the other hand, will be more vulnerable to the vagaries of everyday life no matter how affluent or stable their upbringing.

Four of the best ways you can show your children that you love them are by expressing physical affection, recognizing and praising your child's accomplishments, accepting them for who they are and providing a safe haven for them. So how do you go about showing your love like this? Let's look at these four areas in more detail.

Warmth and physical affection

Hugging your children and telling them that you love them might seem like a no-brainer, but you'd be surprised at how many parents forget to do it on a regular basis.

Warmth and physical affection seem to diminish as a child gets older – just at the time when they need it the most. Studies have shown that both mothers and fathers show less physical affection and warmth towards their children as they grow up. One piece of research measured how often parents hugged their children: when they were under three years old, 90 per cent of parents said they hugged their children every day, but by the time they had reached the age of ten, only 75 per cent of the mums and 50 per cent of dads were hugging their children on a daily basis.

But is it really important to show your child warmth and physical affection? Many people from older generations managed without a childhood filled with hugs and kisses, so has the 'seen-and-not-heard' approach to parenting done them any harm? Plenty of studies reveal that warmth in the parent-child relationship is vital and that children who are shown love in this way tend to have higher self-esteem, better parent-child communication and fewer psychological and behavioural problems. Parental warmth and affection have also been linked to better academic success and developing problem-focused coping styles. Lack of parental warmth, on the other hand, seems to encourage feelings of alienation, hostility and aggression, as well as poor self-esteem and antisocial or risky behaviour.

Physical affection isn't just wonderful for your children – it's also great for you. Physical bonding is a huge part of being a parent and your love for your child can only increase with regular physical contact. Think how lovely it is to have a baby fall asleep in your arms or to receive a spontaneous hug from your teenager. Remember, too, that physical contact is also a great stress reliever.

Showing physical affection as your child grows up

Most parents don't have a problem expressing physical affection when their child is a baby because then you spend a great deal of time holding them, carrying them around or feeding them close to your body. Even playtime and bath-time are physical – with lots of kisses, cuddles and tickling. Babies love this type of physical affection and they thrive on it. In fact, it is so important

for babies to have very high levels of physical affection that when it is absent in the parent-child relationship the consequences can be very serious. Numerous studies (among both animals and humans) have shown that limiting body contact and depriving an infant of human attention can lead to chronic stress, which in turn permanently shapes the stress responses in the brain.

Kiss it and make it better
When children hurt themselves or are frightened, hugs and cuddles from you help to release endorphins in them – chemicals in the brain that are responsible for good moods and natural pain-relief.

As your child grows up and becomes more physically independent, you will need to create opportunities to be physically affectionate and also learn to recognize when your child doesn't want to be smothered in hugs and kisses. Parents often find that when their child reaches school age they start to resist attempts at physical affection and might balk at the idea of having to give you a kiss or resist being cuddled in public. This is not because your child has stopped loving you – while the first few years of your child's development are focused on developing a close relationship between parent and child, the early school years see children practising feelings of independence and autonomy. As a result, sometimes displays of physical affection make your children feel as if you are still treating them like a baby, when they want to feel 'grown up'. This is a tricky dilemma because young children still need physical affection. The answer is to learn more subtle ways of displaying physical affection that won't embarrass them or undermine their feelings. Tell them that you love them and that they are very important and special. Even if they resist a hug, you can still show affection through positive physical touch – by hand holding, or by placing an arm around the shoulder or a kiss on the head as you buckle them into the car.

The key to this new independence is often public versus private: your children may still enjoy hugs and kisses at home, but don't want them in front of their school friends. Take your lead from them. This 'stop embarrassing me' phase can carry on well into adolescence; however, once children grow up and feel confident that the world sees them as adult, they often go back to allowing their parents to demonstrate physical affection in public.

Physical affection and boundaries

Some adults feel awkward about showing warmth and affection to a child. This may be because they themselves never received affection as a child and therefore feel uncertain where to start, or perhaps because that they feel uncomfortable with their child growing up and developing sexually.

Increasing awareness of the problem of child sexual abuse has also caused some parents, especially fathers and stepfathers, to question whether it's OK to cuddle their children. The answer is, of course, a resounding yes! Children of all ages not only want but need physical affection from their parents. It is perfectly natural to cuddle, hug and kiss your children in a non-sexual way. Be aware that older children might not feel as comfortable about physical affection as younger ones, so the key is to listen to your child and respect their wishes at every stage.

Recognition and praise

Your child will feel good if they are told that they are good. The best way to do this is to recognize their achievements and give them lots of praise. Praise and recognition are important to all children – they allow them to develop a view of themselves as loved and lovable. They also build confidence and self-esteem, encourage them to take on new challenges and give them the emotional resilience to bounce back if things go wrong.

How to praise your children

Children pick up on atmosphere and tone more than you would think. When you give praise, make sure that your tone and facial expressions match what you are saying. Children also need to know what exactly it is that they did right. Use their name, look them in the eye and be specific – 'Ben, you tidied your room. Well done!' or 'Sarah, you did a great job on your homework.'

You can never praise too much: the small successes are just as important as the big ones. Cleaning their teeth or behaving nicely at the supermarket are just as worthy of praise as doing well at school. Praise with a sting in its tail isn't real praise. Saying things like 'You look nice today – pity you're scruffy the rest of the time' or 'Well done for getting a B – shame it wasn't an A...' will make your child feel criticized, not praised.

Children showing love back

Little children have no qualms about showing physical affection. However, as your child grows up they might find it difficult to express their love for you in a physical way. If you are worried by the fact that your child isn't as physically affectionate as they used to be or you'd like them to be, remember that children show their love in lots of different ways. All of the following behaviours are a child's way of telling their parents they love them, without necessarily saying it.

Treasure and encourage these moments as much as the hugs and kisses:

■ Helping you out in various ways.

■ Copying you or learning from what you do.

■ Wanting to be physically near you.

■ Sharing their experiences or feelings.

■ Telling a joke or funny story.

■ Putting on a performance – a play, a song or a dance.

■ Making you little gifts or drawing you a picture.

Praising children solely for their academic performance can lead them to believe that only good test results matter. While this praise is often given by parents and teachers with the best intentions, it seems that it leaves children ill-prepared to cope when failure strikes. One American study compared children who were praised for their intelligence with a group of children who were praised for their effort. The research found that complimenting children for their intelligence alone makes them highly performance-oriented but also extremely vulnerable to setbacks. Children who were commended for their effort, on the other hand, concentrated on the value of learning and strategies for achievement.

It seems that children who are praised for their inborn abilities when they are successful (for example, 'Michael is naturally good at Maths') begin to believe that intelligence is fixed at birth and isn't something that can be developed or improved. When they then fail at something (which will happen to all children at some time), those children believe that it must be due to their own lack of intelligence, and their self-esteem takes a huge knock. Children who are labelled as 'gifted' are particularly prone to this problem – having relied on their natural ability and never having been taught the value of trying hard.

The most beneficial type of praise, therefore, focuses on effort and hard work. When children are taught the value of trying hard, they can deal with challenges and setbacks when they happen and they also won't feel that failure is something inherent in who they are; rather that it's just another obstacle to overcome. When your children do well, the praise should be about how they did their work, rather than about the grade or test result they achieved. This is the 'you tried really hard, I'm really proud of you' school of praise. That's not to say that we can't praise our children for their natural talents, just that we should be careful not to rely solely on this form of compliment. Honesty, independence and kindness are just as important and praiseworthy as demonstrating a natural aptitude for something.

Another important point to remember about praise is that it should never be given in comparison with someone else. Parents often take great pride in measuring their children against others, but you have to remember that competition at school is tough enough without parents piling on further pressure. You need to judge your child for their own achievements, not because they did better or worse than their peers. Setting siblings against each other is particularly unhelpful, and can lead to years of family resentment.

Accepting your child for who they are

This section could equally be called 'unconditional love'. It's important that we accept our children for who they are, not what we would like them to be. Parents often have high expectations that their children will fulfil a certain role – you hear often mums and dads saying, 'He's going to be a world cup player' or 'She's going to be a heartbreaker when she grows up'. While it's lovely that parents have high hopes for their offspring, it's important that these hopes don't become an overwhelming burden for your child.

Hot topic Criticism

Part of loving your child is understanding how to deal with them when they don't behave well or don't fulfil your expectations. A whole chapter could be written on criticism, but there's one point that stands out above all the others: criticize the behaviour, not the child. Children need to be told when they have done something wrong but the focus should always be on the child's actions, not on them as a person. Tell your son it was wrong for him not to do his homework, but don't call him a lazy so-and-so. Similarly, explain to your daughter that you are cross because she stayed out late and you were worried, and don't tell her that she's a bad, selfish person.

Criticizing your child and not the action undermines their confidence and self-esteem. Children who are persistently criticized can end up believing that they are inherently bad people and often feel that there is no point trying to be good.

Remember, too, not to make fun of your child. Parents shouldn't mock their children or make fun of them in a cruel way – not only is it hurtful, but if it is done in front of other people it can humiliate and embarrass them. Even worse, if it's done behind their back and they find out, the child will feel doubly bad because they have been criticized and deceived.

Hot topic Birth order

Where do you come in the sibling pecking order?

Some theories have suggested that our position in the sibling pecking order can have an impact on our personality, ambitions and successes in life. This theory tends to apply most when the age gaps between siblings are less than three years. Does this ring any bells with your family?

First child

As the 'pioneer' offspring, they initially enjoy undivided attention from their parents. When the second child comes along, first children can feel threatened. They attempt to regain their position in the family by working hard to please their parents while attempting to control younger siblings. As a result, first-borns tend to be high-achievers, conscientious and look for positions of power and authority.

Youngest child

They are seen as the baby of the family, even as an adult. On the one hand it's great to feel pampered, on the other it can be stifling never to be viewed as fully grown up. Given greater freedom and un-burdened by high parental expectation, last-borns often choose an interesting, very individual life path. The youngest child in a family is often the most easy-going and liberal-minded, but they also can find it difficult to make decisions and take responsibility.

Middle child

Middle children often complain that they have the worst of both worlds: they can be unpopular with the first-born child (who views their arrival as a threat), and yet never enjoy the benefit of being the youngest. Middle children end up being the 'peacemakers' between older

Managing expectations

The first thing to do to put your expectations into context is to accept that your children are different from you and therefore they will not share your hopes and fears and will probably want to follow their own life path. Your job is to help your child to grow up to fulfil his or her own potential. It is important that you communicate the idea to your child that you love them, regardless of what they want to do as a career or how well they do at school.

and younger siblings as they are great at adapting to different situations and make natural diplomats. Unfortunately, they can also feel insecure about their place and importance within the family and feel that life is inherently unfair.

Only child

Only children share many characteristics with first-borns but, as they never have siblings, they often end up preferring the company of adults or wanting to be by themselves. This may mean that they have poor peer relations as a child, but these tend to improve as they get older. Only children often have to entertain themselves, which can make them very creative and imaginative people. Only children also tend to make very confident adults.

Parents often live vicariously through their children – encouraging them to achieve in areas where the parents would like to have succeeded themselves. This kind of pressure can be unbearable for a child: not only do they feel that they have to achieve a certain goal that is not of their choosing, but they also feel that they will be letting the family down if they fail. Other parents put a strong emphasis on one type of success – academic, financial, sporting and so on – without appreciating whether this type of success is appropriate or important to their child. Take the time to get to know your child and understand what is important to them. Encourage them without forcing them in a particular direction.

Accept that children learn differently

An offshoot from the idea of accepting your child for who they are is acknowledging that children have different strengths and learn differently. Some children have a natural aptitude for visual or abstract concepts, whereas others learn more quickly through interaction and physical tasks. (Find out more about the different ways children learn in Chapter 4.)

Learning 'difficulties' are also more common than parents might imagine. About one in ten children has dyslexia – mainly boys, but it also affects a large number of girls – and it's thought that 345,000 children in the UK now have problems with hyperactivity or keeping their attention on something. As a parent, you need to recognize and appreciate that children do not all learn in the same way and will have different strengths and weaknesses from you.

Accepting differences within the family

This philosophy extends into all different types of behaviour. Individual children within one family can be extraordinarily different – they can develop varying food preferences, hobbies, pastimes, friendships, temperament, sexuality: everything can be different from their siblings. Sometimes this comes from inherent characteristics, or sometimes it's due to subtle differences in parenting – even their order of birth can affect your child's personality and life direction (see Hot topic: Birth order on pages 102–3). What is important is that your child knows they are normal, and that it's normal to be different. This will also help them respect differences in others.

Providing a safe emotional environment

Parents spend a lot of time worrying about their child's physical environment at home, but how many of us pay attention to their emotional environment?

Part of being a loving parent is providing your child with a safe haven. Children often find the outside world – school and friendships, for example – quite tough. It's really important that they feel they have a home where they can come back, relax and know that, however bad things get, they have a place of love and respite. The best way to arrange this is to try to make sure that family members treat each other with kindness and respect. In particular, it's important that children don't have to witness their parents constantly arguing or bickering. Various studies have shown just how harmful it is for children to live in houses filled with conflict and unpredictability, especially for any protracted length of time. Children of warring parents are more likely to experience mental and behavioural problems, such as depression, anger and anxiety. They may also find it difficult to have positive relationships when they become adults themselves.

Unfortunately, all relationships go through rocky patches and some can end in separation and divorce. If there is this sort of disharmony in your family, it's important to try to resolve issues calmly and in private, limiting the impact that your marital problems have on your children. Family mediation or counselling can be really helpful in guiding parents and children through family breakup or to find ways of reconciling differences.

Even if your relationship isn't going through a crisis, it's worth remembering that children learn about adult relationships from what they see in the home. How do you relate to your partner? Do you show love and affection to them on a regular basis? Do you spend quality time together? As with every aspect of parenting covered in this book, being a good role model is half the battle. Children learn so much from their parents and teaching them how to relate to others is one of the greatest tools you can give them for later life.

Kris's Top Tips

Remember every child is unique

Spend time with each of your children, alone and get to know them properly. Let them know that you value them as individuals and avoid talking about their siblings during this one-to-one time.

Show them affection

Hug, kiss and tell your children that you love them every day. Children of all ages thrive on physical affection.

Praise a job well done, however small

Whether it's making the netball team or setting the table nicely, focusing on effort, not just results, will really boost their self-esteem and confidence.

Make them feel good

Lots of children worry that they are a burden to their family or that their parents resent them being there. Tell your children how much you enjoy being their parent and how glad you are to have them in your life.

Don't give things in place of love

You can't spoil your child with too much love; however, you can spoil them with things given in place of love, such as indulgent rule-bending or showering them with material possessions.

Let them show you that they love you

Treasure the paintings, models and other artwork they make you. Pin them up on the fridge or make a special display in a prominent place. Be a good audience for their songs or dance routines.

Criticize the behaviour, not the child

Children should be told when they do something wrong, but focus on the child's actions not them as a person.

Make your home a safe haven

Keep the atmosphere in your house as warm and caring as possible. Create an environment where your children can escape from the pressures of the outside world.

Be a role model

Make time to keep your own relationship strong and set a good example by being loving and affectionate with other family members. If children see parents expressing their own discontent by yelling at each other, they are more likely to use those tactics themselves.

Avoid making comparisons

Comparing siblings can often fuel resentment. If one child has behaved badly, don't tell them they should be good like their sister or brother. Equally, if they have done well, don't say that they are better or cleverer than their sibling.

Other types of family stress can have a negative impact on children. Work or financial worries often have a habit of seeping into family life, and while children can't and shouldn't be shielded from everything that's worrying in life, the home should be a calm, restful place and not an extension of the office. If you work from home, try to keep your working life separate from home life. Equally, if you work away from home it's important that you try to leave any work pressures at the front door. Predictability is also a crucial factor in providing a safe haven for children. As we talked about in the Sleep chapter (Chapter 3), children find routine very comforting, because it helps them feel in control and confident about what to expect at any moment. Although spontaneity is great once in while, familiarity is more reassuring for a child than endless surprises.

chapter 6

Getting involved

Playing a part, supporting, guiding, communicating and learning enables parents to understand how their children are developing, and makes children feel their parents are interested in them. Sounds simple, but nowadays it seems there are increasing pressures on us to cram more into our already busy life, and it can be hard to make family time.

Why is getting involved so important?

We've mentioned this before, so why devote a whole chapter to it? Simple: it's because it is the most important factor in your child's psychological development. How well you are involved with your child has a very strong bearing on their mental health, how well adjusted they are and their long-term happiness. This is true whether your child is three months old, three years old or 13.

How does this involvement affect your child?

Children with involved parents will typically:

- Perform better in school.
- Feel better about themselves.
- Be less likely to develop emotional problems.
- Be less likely to take risks and get into trouble.

Getting involved is about much more than just asking your child questions about things. Most parents are familiar with the way that conversations with children of any age (and not just with teenagers) can sometimes turn into interrogations:

You: How was school today, Jamie?
Your child: It was OK.
You: What lessons did you have?
Your child: Maths and French.
You: Did you pass that tables test?
Your child: Yep.
You: Did you hear that Robbie Williams has learnt to fly just by flapping his arms up and down?
Your child: Nope.
[Pause...]
Your child: Er... What's for tea, Mum?

At times, getting children to open up on just about any subject can be difficult, or verging on the impossible. Remember that children tend to choose carefully their moments to open up, just as adults do. You might not know when those

What does 'getting involved' really mean?

The simplest answer is to do the following exercise:

1   First, write a list of all of the activities that your child takes part in where you don't know exactly what they do in that time. Be honest with yourself – the list is for your benefit only. Here are some possible examples:

- Lessons at school.
- Activities after school.
- Homework.
- Playing with friends.
- TV and computer games.
- Books they're reading.

Once you've finished, take a careful look at that list. If you're surprised at just how much your child does that you know little or nothing about, don't make yourself feel bad – you're in exactly the same boat as most parents.

However, now is the time to do something about it. For every one of the activities listed above, ask yourself two questions:

- How you can find out more about what's involved?
- How can you play a part in it?

2   Next, make a similar list that includes how your child thinks and feels about all the major parts of their life. Again, write down the things that you really don't know much about – and be honest – such as:

- How happy they are at home.
- How happy they are at school.
- How they feel about themselves.
- If they feel they have enough friends and people to play with.
- How they feel about their family (you included).
- What they are interested in, or would like to try.

Then, for each of these areas, think about how to best talk to them about it.

NB – One important point: remember that children – especially older ones – need privacy just like adults. Give them space, and don't make them feel as if you're spying on them.

moments will be, but the more involved you are in your child's life, the more likely it is that you'll be there when it happens.

Being involved – how it changes over time

The way we involve ourselves in our children's life should change steadily and constantly over the years. Up to the age of three or four years old, much of our involvement is about carefully controlling an activity to make sure that it is safe and enjoyable for the child. But as he or she gets older, parents find that they can 'relax the reins' a little more as children start to understand safe ways to do things. All of this could apply to homework, play or learning a new skill. When a child turns into a teenager these reins must be relaxed a little more – to the extent that the child can really begin to experiment and find things out for themselves, as well as learn to take responsibility for situations when their parents aren't in control.

There's an important principle behind all of this. 'Relaxing the reins', which is a necessary and healthy part of allowing your child to grow up and be more independent, does not mean 'not being involved'. Many parents think that the best way to let children learn as they get older is simply to leave them to it. This approach is OK in small doses, but there should never be a time when you are not involved at all in your child's life.

Making time – and guarding it carefully

The majority of parents would say that they lead a busy life; there isn't a lot of spare time for a start, and we often feel as though it's a struggle to fit everything in. Lots of activities (both practical and enjoyable) are rushed as we try to get to our next commitment on time.

Something else happens when parents are busy, too. We *multitask*: we feed the baby while we're on hold to the electricity company, or we have a bath while she's asleep. Later on we might grab something to eat in between going to the supermarket and doing the school run, or we sneak a quick nap while our children are watching their favourite DVD. We multitask because it saves us valuable time, but multitasking has a downside, too. When we're so used to

How to allocate and guard time with your children

- 'Fence off' time with your children hours, days or even weeks in advance.

- Treat that time with the same commitment that you would a meeting at work or something equally important. Mark it in your diary if necessary.

- Tell friends, family and work about it if you have to, to make sure they know you can't be anywhere else but home at that time.

- Turn off your mobile and turn on the answerphone. Don't let calls distract you from your children – except in genuine, serious emergencies.

- Work does not count as an emergency – unless you work for the emergency services. If once every few months you have to rearrange a family outing for work, that's OK, but more often than that and perhaps you need to rethink your priorities.

- Working from home is increasingly common. The fact that your whole life is in one place makes it harder to draw a clear boundary between work and family life. Be rigid about what is work time and what is family time.

doing two things at once, we can easily forget that there are times when we need to give our full attention to our children.

A perfect example of this is setting aside time for an activity with your children – usually in the evenings and weekends. If you don't give your full attention to that activity, children are surprisingly good at picking up on it. This has two consequences – first, your child doesn't enjoy the activity as much (because they're not really interacting with you), and second, they feel disappointed that what they thought was going to be 'family time' is being eroded. As a general rule, don't be tempted to fool your children into thinking that they have your full attention when they don't. Multitasking is an unavoidable fact of life at times, but children can often sense when we're not totally focused on them. If we try to conceal this, our children find it confusing and disappointing when they realize the truth – and ultimately they can lose faith in us.

Hot topic Quality time

Spending time with your children – quality not quantity?

It's a thorny question. In the late 1980s a parenting approach referred to as 'quality time' became increasingly popular. This idea began in the US but it has recently been widely adopted in the UK. What this theory suggested was that it was OK to spend less time with your children as long as what time you did spend with them was quality time. This seemed to suggest that somehow certain activities or ways of interacting with your children were more valuable than others, and as long as you filled your time together with those 'quality' activities, everything would be fine.

Essentially, this theory has become popular because of the increasing work demands on parents in both the US and the UK. Most western countries work longer hours, have lower unemployment rates and have more women working than ever before. (This is probably truer of the UK than almost any other country in the world.) The pressure on parents to juggle work life and family life has never been greater, and so the quality-time idea was attractive to many parents because it seemed to say that they shouldn't feel guilty about spending less time with their children.

So does the quality-time theory hold any truth? Well, it does in one sense: two people (whether parent and child, or two

adults, or two children) can spend hours or even days in each other's company without really interacting, communicating, learning about each other or being involved in each other's life. What happens during that time is the crucial thing. BUT – and it's an important but – there is a limit to how much any relationship, and particularly a parent-child relationship, can be compressed into short bouts of 'quality time'. This extra pressure can in fact cause more harm than good.

A strong argument for increasing the quantity of time spent with your child is that this is a particularly important factor when it comes to communication. As we pointed out earlier, children on the whole don't like feeling pressurized to communicate – they like to take their time, and choose their moment carefully to say what's on their mind. The only way to make sure that you're there for them to talk to is by spending a quantity of time with them.

So the long and short of it is that it is equally important to devote a sufficient quantity of time to interacting with your children – you can't simply make up for a lack of quantity by increasing quality.

Working parents

Work can often be an obstacle that prevents parents from getting involved.

In most families, one or both parents have to work. Research shows that children whose mothers work full-time during the first five years of their children's life tend to perform less well at school and are more likely to be unemployed or experience psychological distress in early adulthood. These patterns are more likely to affect boys than girls, but are less likely to occur in children of mothers who work part-time. This doesn't mean that mums shouldn't work full-time. In many families, and particularly in single-parent ones, mums don't have a choice. However, it does mean that often there is a price to pay for spending less time with your children when they are very young and that you should consider this carefully if you're planning to have children and work full-time. On the upside, children under the age of five who attend nurseries are often more socially confident, as they have had to learn to be more self-reliant.

If you are a working parent, and your employer is pressuring you to work hours that leave you with no family time, you can do something about it:

■ Talk to your employer: tell him or her about the time pressure you're under and how it is adversely affecting your family life. Despite the longer hours that many of us work these days, many employers are sympathetic to the demands of family life.

■ The law states that employers must offer flexible working wherever possible, and it is becoming an accepted practice in many organizations. It may mean keeping the same overall hours but at different times, or reducing your hours along with your pay, or working from home for a certain number of days a month.

■ 65 per cent of women with dependent children are in work – this compares to 89 per cent of men. But the gap between those two figures has been narrowing for many years.

■ More than half of all parents who work full-time are worried that they spend too little time with their family.

A great many employers now understand that it is actually in their interests to allow a trusted employee to alter their working hours to make their home life easier. Find out your company's policy on flexible working hours, then ask for an open discussion about the possibilities.

■ The European Working Time Directive (WTD) is a strong and binding piece of legislation which aims to protect employees from exploitation by employers – particularly when it comes to working hours. Most important, the WTD states that no employee should be forced to work more than 48 hours per week. UK employers do have an opt-out clause, so you'll need to find out your company's position on it before you take action. (See Further resources.)

■ In extreme cases, and if you've tried all other avenues, consider finding a new job. Leaving a secure position is one of the hardest things a working parent can ever do, but not spending enough time with your children has an equally difficult impact. In some cases, leaving a job may be the only way to change that situation.

Getting involved in your children's schooling

In Chapter 4 we looked at some of the ways in which you can get involved in your children's education – including helping them with their reading and their homework. Here, we're going to look at getting involved in their schooling.

Home-school agreement

If you already have children in school, this is something you might already be acquainted with. The home-school agreement typically looks like one or two pages of a contract which sets out the responsibilities of the school, the parents and, of course, the child. Most schools have one that all parties must sign when the child joins the school.

The home-school agreement was introduced in the mid-1990s and the idea behind it was to encourage parents' involvement in their children's schooling. The agreement typically includes:

■ When a child is expected to attend school and the basic principles of behaviour while at school, for instance, punctuality, effort in schoolwork, due consideration for others and so on.

■ Parents' basic commitments, such as getting their children to school on time, attending open evenings and informal meetings, helping with homework and providing notes in the case of absence.

■ The parents' expectations of the school, in terms of basic standards of education, addressing special needs and keeping children safe.

Home-school agreements offer parents a good grounding to get involved with their children's schooling. Read your agreement carefully and spend a little time thinking about how best you can fulfil your side of the bargain.

Other ways of getting involved with your child's school

There are LOADS of ways in which you can get involved with your child's school. On the whole, schools appreciate all the help and involvement they can get from parents, so try to make a little time to join in on some of the following:

Open evenings

A good way to find out more about what's happening in the school – and they can often be relaxed and fun occasions.

Plays and concerts

If your child is in a school play or concert, make every possible effort to be there, as it usually means a lot to your child.

Sports days

These events can be great fun and, again, if your child is competing, do make every effort to be there. Sports days are often during the day so they can be harder for working parents to attend, but it's a really fun, sociable day out when you can also chat to both their teachers and other parents.

Helping out on school trips

Many schools welcome parents along on school trips to help out as an extra pair of responsible hands. It might mean a trip to a farm, a museum, or later on perhaps the theatre. You'll usually have a great day out yourself, as well as contributing to it for the children.

Governors' meetings

These are a good place to raise any concerns that you might have about the way the school is being run (as opposed to specific issues you may have re-garding your own children), as well as finding out about any major changes that might be happening in your school, such as amalgamations, curriculum changes and relocations.

Parent teacher associations (PTAs)

Although PTAs don't usually have formal powers, they're one of the best options you have for finding out about what's really going on in your children's schools. You'll be able to discuss issues and problems with both parents and teachers, and often in a setting that enables you to have your say in a way that wouldn't be possible at a more formal event.

Getting involved with your children's social group

This doesn't mean following your child around every second of the day, but as a parent you have a responsibility to show an interest in your child's social life and be aware of how they spend their leisure time. This isn't because parents should be constantly checking up on their children, but it can help to prevent your child getting into trouble as a result of having friends who are a bad influence. Your child will choose his or her own friends. Peers are important and influential in your child's life, and by the time they reach secondary school your children will probably be spending more time with their friends than with you. You cannot choose your child's friendship group (much as you might like to at times) and you can't tell your child what to think, but you can make a big difference to how much your child will be influenced by those peers. Children who have an open and warm relationship with their parents will feel more able to discuss problems that arise, which will also make them less likely to succumb to negative peer pressure. Later on in this book you will find a chapter about communication: this is the best way to ensure that your child has the emotional tools to deal with any unwanted peer pressure or risky situations.

It's also important to try to limit the amount of unstructured times your children spend out with their friends – chances are it will be spent roaming the streets or gathering in groups, neither of which are conducive to good behaviour. As a general rule, always try to follow the 'three Ws' rule – know *who* they are with, *where* they are, and *when* they'll be back. That way, you can relax knowing that your child is safe and has enough freedom to grow and develop as an independent person.

Make time for yourself, too

After everything we've said about spending more time with your children, it might seem a strange piece of advice to give – but keeping time aside for both you and your partner is a critical part of parenting.

■ No parent needs to be told that bringing up children is stressful. We all need time that is ours to control – a little space in which to unwind and to do the things that make us happy as individuals, rather than as parents. If we are happy in ourselves, we are happier parents.

■ Relationships need regular attention to stay healthy. Make sure that at least once a week you and your partner spend time together without the children. Any expense that you incur (such as a babysitter) is worth every penny. A happy, healthy relationship makes for a better set of parents.

■ Absence makes the heart grow fonder – and in measured quantities this is absolutely true. Spending time apart from your children can make you miss them and look forward to seeing them that little bit more. Your children will feel the same way too, as having an occasional short break from their parents reminds them how much you do for them and how much they love you.

Try not to think of time away from the children as a luxury – it's a necessity. This doesn't mean leaving your children to fend for themselves for long stretches of time, but it does mean being kind to yourself and finding a way to relieve the pressure that family life can create.

Kris's Top Tips

- There's no substitute for spending a good quantity of time with your children.

- Mark out some time for your children and don't let distractions get in the way.

- If there are areas of your children's life you feel you know little about, make it your goal to find out. Ask gentle questions, but don't pressure them.

- Get as deeply involved with your child's school as you can. Attend all evenings to discuss your child's academic performance, and pop along to PTA and governors' meetings if you have time.

- If your child's school has a home-school agreement, take it seriously. It's a good checklist for being involved with your children's education, and will tell you what you have a right to expect from the school.

- Maintain a strict distinction between work time and family time.

- If you are your child's main carer, investigate all your options before working full-time and try to find a balance between work and home life.

- As your children grow up they'll want more freedom and more privacy. This does not mean that you should stop being involved in their lives.

- Take time out for yourself. It'll make you a calmer and happier parent.

chapter 7

Discipline and boundaries

Talk to ten different parents and you'll get ten different views about discipline. At one end of the scale you have parents who believe that smacking is the only way, and at the other end you'll find mums and dads who set few boundaries and let their offspring do as they please. We all want our children to behave well, so who has got it right?

Why boundaries are important

The first thing to say about discipline is that it is important. Children need to be loved – most parents agree on that – but they also need boundaries. Many parents are reluctant to enforce discipline because they don't want to be unpopular with their children, particularly if they remember the discipline they received in childhood and feel that it was unnecessary or harmful.

The reality is that all children need boundaries, and if they cross over these boundaries they need to be disciplined. As adults we may think that the idea of living by rules and limits is unpleasant, but the truth is that children need and thrive on boundaries. They need to know what behaviour is acceptable and what is not and this kind of moral structure, far from making a child feel uncomfortable, actually makes them feel secure. In the same way that routines make children feel safe and protected, so clearly defined boundaries help your child to make sense of the world.

As an adult you need to be able to control your own behaviour. In all social interactions we have unwritten rules about what's appropriate and what's not. Adults who have not learned the rules and limits of social behaviour find interacting with others problematic. People who are very impulsive, demanding or aggressive, for example, often find that they don't relate to others and find it difficult to form friendships or relationships.

Children learn these boundaries while they are growing up. As a parent, your job is to set and enforce these rules so that, as your children become more independent, they can start to develop their own sense of internal control. By the time they are teenagers, the role of imposing control has gradually moved from you to the children themselves. For example, a young child needs to be told to wash and brush their hair every day, whereas a teenager will do this for themselves without being asked (hopefully!). So, rather than harming your child, by setting boundaries and imposing discipline you are actually helping them to become an independent, well-adjusted adult.

'No' and 'Because I said so!'

So why do we have to learn to say no to our children? It can seem cruel to deny your child something that they want, and no one likes to be the bad guy, but no is a useful word and one that is essential for good discipline. You need to say no to your child at a young age so that later in life he or she can say no to himelf or herself. If you can't say no to yourself as an adult, your life will be driven by whim and impulse and you will find it difficult to delay gratification, falling victim to the 'I want it now' syndrome.

Although no is a negative word, it can be used to teach your child positive lessons. It's a powerful word, however, so it's important to learn how to use it properly. The key is to strike a balance: if all your child hears is the word no, it can be very frustrating and dispiriting for them. However, if their day is full of the word yes, the first time they hear no it will come as a great shock and you're guaranteed to have a battle on your hands. In reality, the world is full of both no and yes, so you need to reach a compromise.

If you find yourself constantly saying no at home, it might be worth chang-ing your environment and taking your child somewhere where it's easier to say yes. If you are worried about your child hurting themselves at home when they are playing, for example, take them to a soft play centre where they can experience greater freedom and you can enjoy giving them that freedom without worry.

One of the problems with no is that it offers little explanation as to why a certain behaviour is not allowed. Rather than using the ubiquitous 'because I said so' as an explanation (which tells your child you don't really have a good reason for it), if you can explain your decision, do. Children are naturally inquisitive and will want to know why something is forbidden, so you are much more likely to get your chil-dren to comply if they under-stand what you're trying to accomplish. If you can't think of a good explanation, or your child is endlessly using 'why'?' to delay doing what they are told, it's OK to say, 'Because you will be making me happy if you do so'.

Why children break boundaries

So we know why boundaries are important, but this doesn't prevent children from attempting to break them. Children, just as adults do, like to get their own way. You are bound to have rules and limits your child doesn't like: he or she might not like the fact that they have to go to bed at a certain time, or that they need to do their homework instead of going out and socializing. Children lack the life experience and foresight to understand the benefit of some of life's boundaries. They might enjoy staying up late every night, for example, but do they really understand the consequences of being constantly tired at school? Similarly, schoolwork might be a drag, but the repercussions of letting your child drop out of the school system can be very damaging in the long term.

As a child grows up and becomes more independent, they will develop ways of doing things that differ from your own and they will most likely have different views from you on all manner of topics. A degree of conflict between parents and children is inevitable and is a normal part of family life. Studies have shown that the things parents and children argue about most are household chores, homework, appearance and social life. Rather than try to get rid of conflict altogether (which is practically impossible), the best thing a parent can do is to equip themselves with tools to deal with conflict when it happens. Before we look at how to handle conflict, however, we need to look at the different styles of parenting and what effects they have on children.

What's your parenting style?

The amount of conflict and disobedience in a household can be predicted by observing the parents' relationship with their children. Parenting style can have a profound effect on how the children behave. Over the years, psychologists have identified four broad styles of parenting, which tend to remain consistent throughout the child's life and with any subsequent children. The four different styles of parenting are based on how much the parents try to control the child (also called 'parental demandingness'), and how much they listen to what their child wants ('parental responsiveness').

Parental demandingness is also called behavioural control. It sounds scary but it simply means supervising children, setting boundaries and being prepared to discipline them when they misbehave.

Parental responsiveness means being attuned to their needs, being supportive and being prepared to modify rules as your child moves from one stage to another.

The four styles of parenting that have been identified show different levels of demandingness and responsiveness. The four styles are:

Authoritarian

We've all probably met or heard of someone who is an authoritarian parent. These adults tend to be very demanding, focused on obedience and expect their orders to be obeyed without quibble. This rather old-fashioned style of raising children is also characterized by the parent not responding to what the child wants or to any nuances in a situation. This is the 'do as I say, no questions asked' school of parenting. As punishment authoritarian parents often use emotional control – making the child feel guilty or ashamed – or a physical punishment, such as smacking. This sounds extreme, but it is still a very common form of parenting.

Indulgent

This approach is at the opposite end of the scale from that of the authoritarian parent. Indulgent parents demand very little in terms of behaviour but they are highly responsive to what their children want. These adults tend to accommodate their child's every whim, often in the belief that saying yes to everything is the best way to show their children that they love them. Boundaries and limits are few and far between – indulgent parents tend to let their children do what they please and rarely punish them.

Uninvolved

This type of parent is both undemanding and unresponsive: they don't ask anything of their children and they don't give anything in return – no control, no punishments. Uninvolved parents can appear not to care about their children, and in extreme cases they can even be neglectful.

Authoritative

These parents are both demanding and responsive to their child's wants: they set clear boundaries for their child to follow, but they also listen to their child's wishes. Authoritative parents have no problem in asserting their will when necessary, but they are also open to compromise or rule changing if the situation demands it. These parents will act if a rule is broken but it tends not to be in the form of emotional control or physical punishment. In this style of parenting, rewards are used to encourage and reinforce good behaviour (see below).

Which style of parenting works best?

Studies have shown that the last style of parenting on this list – authoritative parenting – generally seems to be the most successful. Because the child feels listened to, while understanding that there are clear boundaries in place, this type of parenting tends to reduce conflict between parent and child and also helps to establish trust and respect on both sides. Children of authoritative parents also seem to be more socially competent and do better at school, even at an early age.

Children of very strict authoritarian parents, on the other hand, tend to perform moderately well in school and avoid getting into trouble, but they are also more likely to have poorer social skills, self-esteem problems and higher levels of depression. Children from indulgent families tend to be exactly the opposite – they usually have good self-esteem but often perform badly at school and are more likely to get involved with problem behaviour. Those with uninvolved parents fare worst of all: children whose parents are neither demanding nor responsive are most likely to perform badly in all areas. The benefits of authoritative parenting and the negative effects of uninvolved parenting can be seen as early as the pre-school years and can carry on right through adolescence into adulthood.

Getting children to behave

So we can see that a good two-way relationship between parent and child is the foundation for encouraging good behaviour, but how does this translate into everyday life and what do you do when children break rules, as they invariably do?

Encourage good behaviour

We all want well-behaved children who know the difference between right and wrong. Numerous studies have shown that the best way to achieve this is through the use of positive discipline, without having to resort to punishments that hurt a child either physically or emotionally.

Too many theories on discipline rely on the assumption that children are inherently naughty and that the relationship between parent and child is a constant battle of wills. Positive discipline, on the other hand, assumes that there is a loving relationship between child and parent, that children like and want to behave well, and that good behaviour is expected and rewarded.

Children behave at their best when they understand what constitutes good behaviour and why it is important, so rewarding good behaviour helps motivate them to keep on trying. This is the 'carrot' in the carrot-and-stick analogy. Believe it or not, children like to please their parents and the trick is to spot when your child is behaving well and to acknowledge it immediately. Rewarding good behaviour as soon as it happens will help to reinforce it and make your child feel good about themselves. It doesn't have to be anything major; it can be a small thing such as your child clearing the table without being asked or putting away their toys. The reward can be anything – spoken praise such as, 'great job' or 'well done', a hug or kiss, a treat – but the main thing is that your child knows that he or she did a good

thing. Younger children often like rewards, such as an extra bedtime story or eating their favourite meal, while older children might respond better to earning points towards a special toy or a trip out.

Punishing bad behaviour

At the same time, you do need to punish bad behaviour when it happens. The two most effective methods are 'time out' and removing privileges (docking pocket money or being grounded, for example). We shall look at physical punishment and verbal abuse later on, but suffice to say that both these approaches are ineffective at best and downright dangerous at worst.

In any type of punishment, three basic factors are key: first, that the punishment should be directly related to a specific act of misbehaviour, not just because you feel your child is generally naughty; second, that it should be age-appropriate; and third, that you should be consistent.

'Time out'

'Time out' involves removing your child from an activity or a group and putting them on their own for a short period. Choose a place in your home that is free from distractions without being frightening for your child – the corner of a quiet room, a chair or the bottom stair are good options – and call it the 'time out' place.

■ When your child misbehaves, kneel down to their level, look them in the eye and tell them calmly but firmly that the behaviour they have just displayed is unacceptable. Warn them that they will have to sit in the 'time out' place if they continue to behave like that.

■ If your child continues to misbehave, calmly take them to the 'time out' area. As a rule, your child should sit on their 'time out' spot for no longer than one minute for every year of their age – for example, four minutes for a four-year-old.

■ Stay within sight or earshot of your child, but don't get into a discussion with them.

■ If your child gets up before time is over, sit them back down and start the 'time out' from the beginning again.

■ When the 'time out' is over, explain clearly why they were given it and ask

Kids love rewards!

Not all rewards for good behaviour have to be material ones. Try to mix and match social rewards (such as smiles and hugs) and fun activities (such as going to the cinema) with material treats (such as extra pocket money or a toy). Here are a few ideas to get you started:

Social rewards	Fun activities	Gifts and treats
Hug	Cinema visit	Extra pocket money
Smile	Trip to the park	Points towards a big treat
Wink	Baking or cooking	Favourite meal or dessert
Clapping hands	Staying up later	CD or book
Verbal praise	Having a friend to tea	Toy or game
	A sleep-over	

Make a reward board

Using a reward board or star chart is a great way to motivate young children to behave well. They work because they help children to see clearly the effects and results of good behaviour.

Get creative!

You can make your own reward board at home. Be as creative as you like and get the children involved too – the more glitter, paint and colours, the better! The picture can be anything you like, but the key is to have ten circles somewhere in the design that can be filled with a sticker every time your child behaves well. You could draw ten bubbles, ten presents, ten rungs on a ladder or ten smiley faces, for example. Even better, make them have a destination – it could be ten footsteps towards a treasure chest or ten steps to

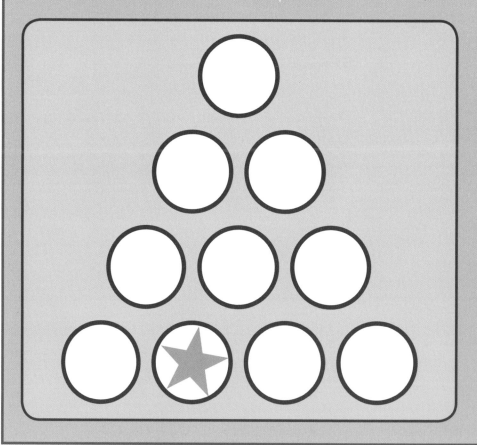

the top of a princess's tower. Once you've designed it, you'll need to buy a couple of packets of brightly coloured stickers. Every time your child behaves well they get a sticker on the reward board. When they have earned all ten stickers, your child gets a reward.

How to use your reward board

■ Decide on the behaviour you'd like to change (for example, tidying their bedroom or helping around the house). Choose only one behaviour at a time.

■ Show your child the reward board and explain how it works. Make it clear which behaviour you want changed and which you are rewarding, for instance, 'You get a star because you tidied your room so nicely – well done!'

■ Put the reward board somewhere very visible – the kitchen wall is ideal.

■ When you put a sticker on the board be very positive and celebrate the event with lots of verbal praise.

■ Never take stickers away. If your child misbehaves and doesn't receive a sticker for a while they will see that they are not getting any closer to their reward target.

them to say sorry. Hug them and then let them leave the 'time out' spot.

■ Amongst pre-school children 'time outs' have been shown to increase compliance with parental wishes by a factor of three, and they continue to be useful as your child grows up. Once your children reach their teens, however, 'time outs' might not be the most appropriate method of punishing bad behaviour and removal of privileges can be more effective.

Removal of privileges

This method of punishing bad behaviour works with children of all ages. Removal of privileges involves withdrawing an activity or facility that the child values, such as going out with friends, pocket money or watching the TV. The removal of privileges teaches a child that his or her actions have consequences and this helps them to take responsibility for their own actions and to think before they act.

The most effective way of removing privileges is to make the punishment relate directly to the misbehaviour. For example, if your teenager insists on staying out late with her friends, even though you have told her you'd like her back at a certain time, the best removal of privilege would be to stop her going out with her friends for a while. A different example might be removing a favourite toy if your child refuses to tidy up her toys or play nicely with them.

A 2004 survey of 630 parents across Britain found that the most popular method of disciplining children was the removal of privileges. Hard smacking was the least popular.

Source: YouGov

When you remove privileges you should make sure that they are ones that matter to your child – there's no point in docking pocket money, for instance, from a child who has a part-time job and earns his own money. Equally, sending a child to his room might not be considered much of a punishment if the bedroom is filled with entertainment such as a computer and a TV. And finally, removing privileges works best if it's for only a short period of time – if children feel that they are never going to get a confiscated item back, they will give up on trying to behave well to get it.

What doesn't work

People discipline their children in lots of different ways. If your children are behaving themselves then surely it doesn't matter which approach you use? In fact, it does. Research has shown that some types of discipline, such as physical punishment and verbal abuse, although somewhat effective in the very short term, don't actually work in the long term. On top of that, these types of harsh punishments can have lasting consequences for both child and parent.

Physical punishment

While physical punishment certainly has an effect on children, it might not necessarily be the one that you were hoping for. Years of research have shown that physical punishment, such as smacking, spanking or hitting your child, has a marked effect on their behaviour, and not for the better. Children who are physically punished learn that hitting someone is an acceptable method of problem solving. Physical punishment is also a significant factor in the development of violent behaviour in childhood and later life.

The effects are the same wherever you go in the world. A global research team recently studied 336 families across six countries – China, India, Italy, Kenya, the Philippines and Thailand – and found that smacking resulted in more behavioural problems in all countries. All the children who were disciplined by smacking showed higher levels of aggression, anxiety and other emotional problems than their contemporaries. Children who are disciplined by corporal punishment are also more likely to go on to be bullies at school and use aggression as a means of problem solving. Children who are aggressive may find it difficult to integrate with children of their own age and are more likely to get involved in problem behaviour and develop conduct issues at school.

Some parents believe that physical punishments, such as a slap, work because they instantly stop bad behaviour. This might be true, but physical punishments don't offer any long-term solution or teach the child why certain behaviour is inappropriate.

Physical punishment is also a risky strategy for disciplining your child because it can get out of control and you could end up harming your child. It can be difficult to control your anger in a moment of crisis and sometimes parents find that they have unintentionally gone too far, whereas other parents find that they need to smack harder and harder over time in order to produce the same result from their children. Hospitals often see cases of what happens when smacking gets out of control and results in more serious harm, such as ruptured eardrums, brain damage and injuries from falls caused by blows. At its extreme end, the devastating statistic is that at least one child every week dies at the hands of their parents or carers in the UK as a result of physical punishment.

Given that there are other more effective strategies for disciplining your children, such as 'time outs' or removal of privileges, isn't it better that you don't take such a risk with your child's wellbeing?

Verbal abuse

Parents can often resort to screaming and shouting to get their children to behave. While we can all lose our temper now and again, using verbal abuse as a regular strategy for discipline can have just as great a negative impact as physical punishment. In fact, children who are regularly verbally abused by their

Hot topic Smacking and the law

The UK law on hitting children has recently been changed: while adults are not allowed to hit each other, a parent is still allowed to smack a child mildly and call it 'reasonable chastisement'. Although it is against the law for teachers, nursery workers and childcare workers to smack another person's child, anyone employed privately by a parent, such as a babysitter or a nanny, may smack a child as long as the parent gives permission to do so. Whoever is doing the smacking, however, may face up to five years in prison if any punishment causes visible bruising, grazes, scratches, minor swellings or cuts.

Most children's organizations, such as the NSPCC, believe that smacking should be banned entirely and in most other European countries, including Sweden, Germany, Italy, Denmark and Austria, children have the same legal rights as adults and there is no defence of 'reasonable chastisement'. But rather than get into the morals of whether smacking should be allowed or not, the primary reason not to smack is that it doesn't work. Research into child behaviour indicates that smacking is not a good way of teaching children the difference between right and wrong. In fact, children who are physically punished are more likely to respond with worsening behaviour or by becoming aggressive. Parents who describe their relationship with their child as less warm and involved are more likely to use smacking as a punishment, and evidence indicates that smacked children are more likely to behave aggressively in later life.

parents can go on to suffer a whole range of problems. Just because a child isn't physically harmed doesn't mean that they don't get hurt.

Not only does verbal abuse cause harm to children, but it actually doesn't work very well as a method of discipline. This is for two reasons: first, because in order to behave well your child needs to believe that you have his or her best interests at heart, and second, the message that you are trying to convey is often lost when you shout and scream.

Children behave best when they feel that you like them for who they are. (See the importance of making a child feel loved in Chapter 5.) Successful parents are those who have children who believe that mum and dad care about their wellbeing above everything else. Children from this type of background trust that the decisions that are made on their behalf (even if they don't like them) come from parents whose intention is to love and protect them. If you constantly shout, scream, humiliate or name-call, your child will soon doubt whether you have his or her best interests at heart. If your child thinks that you don't care, why should he or she follow your rules?

Equally important to bear in mind is that when you try to get something across in an angry way it is very easy for your child to be distracted by the tone of voice rather than hear the content of the message. You might be absolutely right to tell your child that homework is important, but if this message is delivered in an aggressive, hostile manner, your child will fail to see your point and only feel scared or angry in response.

Parents often react to this point and say that it is important to be firm. Yes, being convincing and clear about what you want is very important, but, in truth, that happens best when you are calm and controlled, not when you

Managing anger

All children have the potential to try your patience – it's what they do. When you feel yourself getting angry, the first thing to do is take a deep breath. Count to five slowly or repeat a calm word such as 'relax' to dissipate any angry feelings and let your heartbeat slow. If necessary, take time out for yourself and come back to the situation once you've calmed down.

However, if you feel that anger is a real problem in your family relationships, consider asking for help from a family counsellor or try attending anger-management classes. Your GP will be able to put you in touch with local counselling services, many of which specialize in family problems and dealing with anger.

Regular exercise helps to maintain a sense of calm, as do relaxation exercises and yoga, and meditation will help to release tension in a controlled, healthy way. Diet also plays a part in anger as hunger can trigger feelings of irritability, and so too can excess caffeine and alcohol consumption. Drinking alcohol will also lower your inhibitions, making you quick to anger and to behave more violently.

Kris's Top Tips

Understand that boundaries are important

Far from being cruel to your children, setting boundaries helps them feel secure and safe in the world.

Accept that children will break boundaries

Don't feel disappointed if your children occasionally don't do what you ask them. Children are developing and growing as people, and testing boundaries is one of the ways they learn. All families experience conflict.

Be authoritative

Being too strict or too indulgent with your children isn't doing them any favours in the long term. However, try to balance exerting control with being responsive to their needs.

Be a parent, not a best friend

Sometimes your desire to be popular with your child will be at odds with your obligation to be a good parent – the latter should always win out.

Practise positive parenting

Children are born with a natural desire to please their parents. Rewarding good behaviour and viewing your children as good people is much better than ruling them with an iron rod.

Use reward boards

Let children see the results of their good behaviour – they'll soon work out that it pays to behave!

Don't use physical punishment or verbal abuse

'Time outs' and removal of privileges are the best ways to discipline your child when they misbehave. Negative punishments have poor results and detrimental long-term effects on both parents and children.

Learn to control your anger

Cut out the yelling and shouting and the chances are that your child's behaviour will improve almost immediately.

It's OK to say no

Saying no is an important part of discipline. However, use it carefully and sparingly if you don't want its effect to wear off.

Avoid saying 'Because I said so'

Children will respect and comply with your decisions more easily if they can see the reasoning behind them.

are ranting and raving. Being firm is not the same as being aggressive. When parents are verbally abusive to their children, it is often in a moment of anger, and not because they deliberately want to hurt them. If you tend to let words out before you've had a chance to calm down, take stock and think about what you want to say. Almost all of us could use a little anger management.

chapter 8

Respect and responsibility

This is where children get a pretty bad press. If you believe the media, discipline in schools is now at an all-time low. If children are so much more badly behaved than in previous generations, who is to blame – the parents or the children themselves? How can parents teach children respect for others and the basic principles of good behaviour?

Children and the media

A 2004 poll conducted by MORI turned up some very interesting findings about how children are perceived by the media. MORI combed through 600 of the most recent newspaper articles about young people, identifying whether the article was broadly positive, negative or neutral about them.

■ More than 70 per cent of the articles portrayed young people in a negative light.

■ In tabloid newspapers, 82 per cent of articles were negative.

■ Only 13 per cent of all articles portrayed young people in a positive light.

■ Around 30 per cent of all pieces about young people were about violent crime or anti-social behaviour.

These were extraordinary findings from one of the most respected independent bodies in the UK. They show that the media are very good at portraying the worst sides of young people. But why is this? Perhaps it is because such stories make for more sensational news, or perhaps because they simply reflect what the public thinks of young people. However, the most important question is one that the survey can't answer. To what extent is the media's view of young people correct?

Well, let's look at crime. Most crime is not committed by young people. The vast majority detected crime was committed by over-18s, and most of those were over-21s; but unfortunately, that's not a fact you see reported in the media very often.

Anti-social behaviour

Anti-social behaviour is the term applied to a huge range of activities, of which children are responsible for only a small proportion – the vast majority of anti-social acts are committed by adults.

Respect

When we talk about children and respect, we're often talking about the lack of it – particularly in relation to their elders. Children, like adults, need to respect everyone – not just parents, teachers and other adults, but other children and, of course, themselves too. But what does respect really mean?

Respect isn't easy to define, and has many different components, from what to do when standing at a bus stop next to a pregnant woman, to what to say when a friend tells you his mum and dad are getting a divorce.

Parents just don't have time to teach their children how to behave respectfully in every possible situation that they might encounter. So what's the alternative? Super-principles. These are rules that children can apply to all situations and, if they are followed, should lead to a happy outcome. These are especially important in a situation where the child doesn't know which specific behaviour they should be adopting.

In terms of children showing respect, regardless of whom it is directed at, the super-principle is simple: children should treat others as they themselves would like to be treated.

But what should children respect? Here are the most important things:

Property

Both yours and that of others. Property is important to all of us, but not just because we like to own nice things. For many people, property also has an

emotional value, and is one way that we can express our individual tastes and interests. A good way to teach your children to respect property is to let them have personal possessions from an early age that are theirs and theirs alone, then show your child that you yourself respect their things and their feelings towards them.

Their environment

Here we mean their surroundings – their bedroom, their home, their street, their school, their town and so on. In the society that we live in today, private property tends to get valued more highly than public spaces – but children need to be taught to respect public places, regardless of whether they appear to 'belong' to somebody or not. 'Public property', such as bus stops, shopping centres and schools, belong to us all. For that reason vandalism and littering, no matter how petty, affect everybody who uses that space.

Feelings

It might be yours, or those of your friends or relatives. Empathy is the really important principle here. From as early as possible, children should be encouraged to put themselves in the shoes of others. When a situation arises, carefully explain to your child the feelings and sensitivities of the person involved and encourage your child to empathize with the person and what they are experiencing. Ask your child to think about how they would like to be treated in such a situation, and suggest that they behave in that way towards the other person.

Privacy

Teaching children to respect privacy can be particularly challenging for parents. By the nature of the relationship, it's hard to give children as much privacy as you would demand for yourself. It's you that has to go into their rooms, tidy up, help them get dressed and so on – not the other way round. Even so, the best way to encourage children to value your privacy (and that of others) is to help them have something that is private to them – a diary is ideal (and helpful in many other ways), or a safe box that contains precious belongings that only they have access to. This way, they'll understand how important privacy must be for others, too.

Listening to others

Respecting the opinions of others is something that tends to be more important later in childhood, when children start to form opinions about things
themselves. However, you can teach your children from a very early age to
listen to what you and others have to say. How? Simple – by listening to them.
Don't cut over what they're saying if you can avoid it. It's always worth listening to what your child has to say on a subject and taking it seriously. You don't
have to agree with them, but listening and considering their opinions sends
them the message that what they have to say is important – not just in childhood, but in later life, too. If you don't respect your children's opinions, they will
lose confidence in expressing them. And, above all, never forget that adults can
learn from children also – not just the other way round.

Physical space

Children need to learn as early as possible to respect someone else's body and
physical space. This means not inflicting physical pain on others, or forcing
others to do things they don't want to do. It also means not touching others in
a sexual way that isn't wanted. None of this means that children can't play in
a 'rough and tumble' manner with each other, as almost all siblings and friends
enjoy sometimes; it just means that rough play should take place only when all
the participants are enjoying it, and no-one is likely to be harmed.

Respect between you and your children

We have already talked about how important it is for children to treat others
as they would like to be treated themselves. Exactly the same is true for you –
show your child respect and you're much more likely to get it in return.

Children are born with an innate desire to look up to their parents and be
like them. As they get older, they begin to understand what it is to be a rounded
human being with flaws and faults – and this applies to their parents as much
as anyone. This is a natural process, so don't be afraid to show your children
that you aren't perfect. In time, they'll come to appreciate the truth much
more than any illusion you create for them.

If you find yourself being disrespectful to your children, you should ask
yourself how you lost your authority so that you needed to resort to that kind

of approach. Shouting, saying rude or impolite things and bullying are not behaviours that you want your children to emulate. Some parents use these tactics to prove to their children that they are in charge; however, they are actually more detrimental to your position and show simply that you are throwing your weight around and abusing your power as a parent.

'Talking back'

Parents, like anyone in authority, sometimes wish that their children would simply do as they're told, without questioning it. One of the examples of disrespect that parents say winds them up most is their children 'talking back' to them.

If you are already a parent, ask yourself for a moment how often you use one of these expressions:

- 'Don't talk back.'
- 'Because I said so.'
- 'You'll understand when you're older.'
- 'Don't argue with me.'
- 'Children should be seen and not heard.'

All parents have moments when there isn't time for discussions or arguments about something – it just has to get done. But none of the above expressions is necessary to get the point across. What we really mean when we say these things is, 'I expect you to just fall back and do exactly what I, or anyone older and stronger, tells you to do.' This isn't good for any child. Later in life, they'll feel as though they shouldn't question any decisions at all.

So what should parents do in this situation? The answer is to explain calmly why you've asked your child to do something, and why there is no alternative. Don't assume that your children won't understand your reasons, or that they need to be protected from 'adult reasoning'. In an absolute emergency, where no discussion is possible, of course it's OK to take action immediately, but it's very important that you explain as soon as you can after the situation why you had to act without explanation. The idea behind this approach is that you are making your children feel that they are allowed to know what's going on, and there is a reason for an action, even if it comes after the event. If you take time to do this, your children will trust you to do the right thing in future emergencies.

Handling emotions

Children very often get emotional about things that adults don't – whether they're angry, afraid, or just upset. It's essential that parents take their children's emotions seriously, however irrational or over-sensitive they may seem. All parents face 'emergency' moments when they have to tell their children to calm down, or stop and think, but that does not mean that you should dismiss their feelings out of hand – always be sensitive to the situation.

Honesty

There are few things worse for children than when they are not believed, especially by someone as important as a parent. Almost all children lie occasionally (as do most adults) – this is a natural part of learning – but parents should never give up believing what their children tell them. It's better to let your child take you for a fool about something once than to assume they are never telling the truth.

Teach by example

Another way to teach our children respect is to show them that we respect others. As with diet, exercise, learning and many other areas covered in this book, children learn a huge amount of their behaviour and attitudes from their parents. If they see you treating others with disrespect, or behaving selfishly in a situation where the considerations of others are important, they'll often do the same. Here are a few examples:

■ **Out and about** – Do you pay attention to others? Do you treat staff in shops and public places with patience and respect?

■ **Authority** – Do you demonstrate respect to figures of authority (such as police, teachers and doctors) through your behaviour and attitudes?

■ **Respect for individual differences** – Do you show respect for people who differ from you (in race, religion, social class and opinions) or are you dismissive of them?

Responsible teaching by example can also help to prevent more serious situations arising. Research suggests that certain types of negative behaviour by parents can significantly increase the risk of their children turning to crime. Those types of behaviour are:

■ **Neglect** – Where parents spend too little time with their children so they simply aren't aware of their children's misbehaviour.

■ **Conflict** – Literally some form of conflict between a parent (or parents) and a child. It could be physical or emotional cruelty, or simply inconsistency, which undermines the respect a child has for their parents.

■ **Deviant parental behaviour and attitudes** – This is all about the example that a parent sets for their child. If parents regularly display contempt for the law, or suggest in some way that law breaking is acceptable, children are very likely to adopt the same attitude.

■ **Disruption** – This is where family life is seriously disrupted, often because of conflict or even a separation between parents.

Responsibility

Respect and responsibility are two sides of the same coin: giving responsibility tends to foster respect. The word 'responsibility' covers a very broad range of things. Of course, the need for children to take responsibility for their actions gets steadily greater as they grow older, and by the time they are adults the hope is that they have become fully responsible and will retain that attitude for the rest of their life.

For young children, here's something that many parents don't realize until too late: children love responsibility. Receiving responsibility shows trust and that they are being treated like a real person (as opposed to a 'half-person' who isn't capable of looking after themselves). It also prepares children for one of those hard but inescapable facts of life – that there are times when something will happen only if you make it happen.

Give your children responsibility from the earliest possible opportunity, under safe conditions. For example, let them:

- Help to feed a baby brother or sister.
- Wash the car.
- Walk the dog.
- Help with a simple part of a meal, such as washing vegetables.
- Buy you something you need from the shops.
- Grow a plant for themselves, and look after it.

Think of your child as someone who is capable of making a useful contribution to the running of the house. However, at the same time, if you are giving your children a new task or responsibility, follow these rules carefully:

■ If at all possible, make it something enjoyable. If your children learn to enjoy responsibility first, you'll find it much easier to get them to knuckle down later to unpleasant tasks that have to be done.

■ Make sure that all necessary safety measures are in place for the particular activity, relevant to their age.

■ If possible, watch them doing something for the first time, but make it clear that you are doing so only to help them get it right – don't forget that children are very good at sensing whether their parents have confidence in them. If they get it wrong first time, don't give up: praise whatever it was about it they did right.

■ As soon as they've got it right, back off and let them get on with it at every opportunity. Backing off is a really important part of responsibility – it's a sign that you trust and believe in them.

■ Unless it's an emergency, or they simply can't get the hang of something (perhaps because they are too young), don't get impatient and take over the task. This is a sure way to lose the value of the exercise.

Independence and decision-making

So far in this section on responsibility I've talked about practical responsibilities, like doing a small job for you, or helping out with a sibling or even a pet. I've explained how this teaches your children to act independently, but there's also another important part of responsibility and independence – decision-making.

The principle here is just the same as for tasks. From as early as possible, allow your child to make decisions for themselves – as long as it is safe to do so – such as:

■ If they're getting ready for an activity or a party, let them plan their preparation – how long it's going to take them, what they'll need to bring, what to wear and so on. If they're way off, guide them, of course, but let them think it all through first.

■ If they're having a friend over, let them decide what games to play and what they are going to do with the time.

■ With a big piece of homework or a project at school, encourage your child to plan it carefully, and think through how to approach it.

It's not about leaving a child to it; there are ways that you can help them make decisions responsibly. For example, in the case of the school project, get them to write down all of the possible angles from which they could approach it, and put a list of 'pros and cons' by each one. At the end, they can have a look at the list and see for themselves which approach will work best.

A little later on, if the family is going on a long walk or perhaps a cycle ride, ask your children to look at the map first and try to work out the best route. Once they've done it – and if you think it's a safe route – take their advice. This is, of course, the most important part of the exercise for a child – testing whether their decision worked in practice. If it does, they'll be chuffed to bits, and if it doesn't, they've learned some valuable lessons for next time.

These are just two examples of how to teach your children to make decisions for themselves, but there are opportunities to do this in just about every part of life – think about instances in your day-to-day routine or at special events that would get them to work something through the way an adult would.

Bad influences

The average secondary-school child spends twice as much time with their peers as they do with their parents. One of the most common worries that parents have as their children grow up is that the influence of these peers may turn out to be negative.

Your child's relationship with their peers is not just about pressure – children tend to seek out friends and acquaintances that they like or admire. In other words, it's about peer preference, not just peer pressure. Many parents, when faced with a discipline problem that is either ongoing or even just a one-off event, will often quickly assume that it is their child's friends who are exerting pressure on them to behave badly, rather than exploring the possibility that their child is actively seeking out troublesome peers.

Recent research has thrown up some predictable findings, such as that children who socialize with smokers will be more likely to take up smoking.

The same is true for drugs, alcohol and criminal behaviour. But the same research also shows that children usually seek out these particular peers, rather than being the victim of pressure from them.

When children are very young, you're likely to spend time with the families you get along with, rather than those that your children choose. But very soon (usually as soon as school begins) it becomes immensely hard for parents to influence whom their child is friends with, and trying to control this is more likely to lead to rebellion than good behaviour. What parents can change, however, is how much their children are led by others.

This brings us nicely on to another of the 'super-principles' that I mentioned earlier. You can't expect to prepare your children for every new situation they'll ever encounter with their peers, but you can teach them this: they must learn to make up their own mind.

Children will always listen to what their peers have to say, but they should be encouraged never to act on the advice of peers without forming their own opinions first. For parents, the overall message is simple – focus your efforts on teaching your children to make good decisions for themselves, rather than worrying about what a bad influence their friends might be.

Kris's Top Tips

- Respect is a two-way street. The best way to get your children to respect both you and others is to **show them respect in the first place**.

- Children should be taught to treat others as they themselves would like to be treated.

- Show respect to others yourself. Don't forget what an important role model you are. How you treat a sales assistant, for example, demonstrates to them how they should behave.

- If you want your children to trust your motives when you tell them to do something, explain to them why it should be done. If it's an emergency or there just isn't time to talk them through a situation, take action anyway, but explain as soon as you can after the event why that action was necessary.

- Children must learn to make up their own mind about things. You won't always be around to help them make responsible decisions.

- The more you try to seem like the perfect parent to your children, the harder it will be for them when they realize that you're not flawless.

- Give children appropriate levels of responsibility from the earliest possible opportunity – but make sure that any necessary safety precautions are in place.

- Don't assume that friends or classmates are responsible for your child's bad behaviour.

- Children get a terrible press these days in terms of respect and responsibility. It's up to you to fight against that by believing in your children and trusting them as much as you can.

chapter 9

Safety

Throughout this book we've talked about providing an emotionally safe place for your children and the importance of providing a haven for them. But just as important as this is creating a safe physical environment. Ironically, sometimes the areas that parents worry about the most aren't always where the greatest risks lie.

What parents worry about

A specially commissioned MORI poll asked parents what worried them the most. Among the top forty answers were quite a lot of concerns about safety, and in particular parents seem to spend a great deal of time and energy worrying about:

- Their child being abducted or murdered.
- Their child being a victim of crime or physical violence.
- Their child being hurt on a school trip.
- Their child being injured in an accident at home.
- Their child being knocked over by a vehicle.

To help parents to decide how concerned they should be about each of these problems, it's best to look at exactly how likely it is for each event to happen, what would happen if the worst did occur, and how much parents can do to prevent it happening in the first place. In other words, we need to understand the concept of risk.

Abduction and murder

If you believed everything that you read in the papers and watched on the TV, you'd be forgiven for thinking that the abduction and murder of children by strangers is a common event. As a result, many parents feel that they have no other choice but to keep their children indoors. This in turn means that, today, most British children have less physical freedom and independence than they did 30 years ago: far fewer play outside and enjoy the unmonitored play that their parents' generation did.

In reality, the likelihood of an individual child being taken by a stranger and killed is tiny – less than five out of 16 million children per year – and while no amount of child murders is acceptable, we have to recognize that the number (fewer than ten children a year) is very small and shows no sign of rising. Compare that figure with the 100 or so children who are killed by vehicles each year, and that puts it into some kind of perspective.

It's also a common belief that girls are more likely to be murdered than boys, and so they experience even more restrictions in what they can do and where they can go. In fact, almost two-thirds of child murder victims are boys.

The depressing reality of these scenarios is that the majority of the children who are murdered each year are usually killed by their parents or close family members, not by strangers. Those at greatest risk are children under one year of age. The strain of looking after a small infant is just too much for some parents, especially if they live in difficult circumstances such as extreme poverty or an abusive relationship. Women who suffer from severe post-natal depression are also at a greater risk of harming their children.

So where does this leave parents? How much should we worry? One conclusion is that rather than focusing on risks posed by random strangers, most families should turn their attention inwards and make sure they are creating a safe, violence-free environment for their children. Key to this is managing our own stress and frustrations, and getting help if we feel unable to cope.

Another thing we should take from all this is that parents who excessively restrict their children's freedom and opportunities for play because of worries about strangers are actually doing more harm than good. Children who are driven everywhere or prevented from exploring the outside world have fewer chances to develop their own independence, interact with peers, or be physically active. The less exercise they get, the greater their chance of developing obesity – the real health risk for children. Ironically, children who are driven everywhere or who haven't had many opportunities to practise being a pedestrian are also at a greater risk of being killed by a vehicle. And finally, on an emotional level, children brought up to believe that the outside world is a dangerous place will not have the confidence or social skills of a child who feels able to cope with new people and new situations.

Physical violence and crime

Violence occurs in all sorts of households – from the richest to the poorest – but the statistics show that when it comes to serious or long-term violence, people who are under stress are most likely to commit the act. This stress often occurs in families where one or both parents are unemployed, on a low income, young, managing by themselves or are part of an unusually large family. Fathers, stepfathers and father-substitutes are also twice as likely as natural mothers to be implicated in the abuse.

The real risk to your children in this instance is you – not strangers. If parents are the people most likely to harm their children, we need to ask ourselves whether we are creating the right environment for them and making sure that we are not resorting to physical abuse when we experience stress.

Physical punishment is also a large source of violence against children (see Chapter 7: Discipline and boundaries). Think about your approach to discipline: can you manage your anger? Are we setting a good example for our children? Teaching them that violence is an appropriate reaction to stress or that it solves problems is not acceptable. If you feel that a situation has got out of control and your children might be at risk, it's time to seek help.

Outside the home one of the biggest threats to children comes from violent bullying. Three out of four men and three out of five women say that they have been physically bullied at some point during their childhood, with some incidents even involving beatings. Violent girl-on-girl bullying has also increased in the past few years.

Bullying should not be seen as an inevitable part of growing up, and you should be aware that such experiences can have long-lasting psychological effects on the victim. Schools are now beginning to take more measures to control the problem, but as a parent there are ways you can help too.

- Talk to your child. Encourage them by saying that you will help them sort out the problem and that you believe them.
- Talk to the school. They have a legal obligation to provide a safe and nurturing environment. Speak to the headteacher or, if that fails to work, take the matter to the school governors.
- Talk to the police. If your child has been assaulted it is a criminal offence and you can make a complaint to the police. They can be very effective at warning off bullies in front of parents.
- For help dealing with bullying, visit Bullying Online at www.bullying.co.uk.

Should you worry about your child being a victim of crime? One in four children say that they have been the victim of some sort of crime in the past year, with the most alarming rise being in low-level street crime such as assaults, muggings and robberies. Most of this street crime is committed by young men against other young men.

The reasons behind such a rapid rise in street crime are unclear – nowadays many children carry high-value possessions such as mobile phones and MP3 players, which might make them more of a target for crime – but we do know that children who are truanting or excluded from school are more likely to become victims of street crime. They are also more likely to become victims of crime in general, so anything parents can do to prevent their child from being out of school during the day will reduce the risk of their being a perpetrator or a victim. Common sense should also lead you to tell your child not to display valuable items in public places, to encourage your child to walk home with other children and to teach your child the basics of personal safety.

School trips

One of the things that parents worry about most when it comes to the safety of their children is their being away from home on school trips. A few tragic incidents in recent years have meant that mums and dads feel nervous about letting their children go away, especially if the trip involves outdoor activities.

However, the reality is that school trips are very safe. Most school children spend at least one or two days away from school premises each year – that's ten million children going on a school trip of some kind every 12 months. On average, three of these children will lose their life on a school trip. While this is clearly three too many, any likely risks involved must be weighed up against the significant benefits of an outing.

By law, school trips have to be closely regulated. A comprehensive risk analysis has to be carried out, and the trip can go ahead only with insurance in place and full parental permission. On top of that, you have to remember that school trips provide a valuable learning experience for children: they allow them to see and practise activities that would not be possible in a classroom environment. On a social level, getting out and about with their peers also helps children to cooperate with one another, to form friendships and to take responsibility for their actions.

If you are worried about your child going on a school trip, why not talk to the school directly about their safety policy for such outings? They should have not only a written policy that you can read, but also a specific plan for the trip. Include questions about the transport to and from the location – one of the

main problems is not the activities on school trips but the fact that children are
ferried around in minibuses or coaches without safety belts. You can also talk
to your children about basic safety rules on the trip – tell them how important
it is to listen to their teacher or group leader, not go wandering off on their
own, and to wear all the appropriate safety gear.

Accidents in and outside the home

Accidental injury is one of the main causes of death for children over the age
of one in the UK – around 300 children every year die as a result of an accident. In fact, more children die each year as the result of accidents than from
major illnesses such as meningitis. Children under five years of age are most

at risk from practically every type of accident. Every year over two million children are rushed into accident and emergency departments, and half of these incidents will have happened in the home. And that's just the accidents that are reported. Parents are the first line of the defence in child accident prevention – you can literally make life-saving decisions for your family.

So what type of accidents do children experience in the home? The most common form of non-fatal injury, by a long margin, is caused by falling. Around 400,000 children every year are whisked into hospital after having some kind of fall – whether it's tripping over or tumbling from a height. Very young children are at the greatest risk of falling off something – whether it's the stairs, a bed or a chair – while boys are slightly more likely to be involved in this type of incident than girls. Swallowing or choking on a foreign body is the second most common cause of accidental home injury, with around 50,000 incidents every year. Around 35,000 children are hurt every year as a result of an accidental burn or a scald, with hot drinks causing the highest number of injuries. A further 25,000 children (mostly under-fives) are treated every year for suspected poisoning – household items such as cleaning materials, medicines, alcohol and garden sprays are often to blame.

The most common form of fatal accident inside the home is a house fire, which, thankfully, claims much lower numbers than any of the other accidents. Even so, around 30 children die every year as a result of house fires.

From the age of seven, children spend a greater proportion of their time outside the home and as a result they are much more likely to have an accident away from mum and dad. Of these, accidents at school are surprisingly common, with around 350,000 children being injured during term time every year. Other 'hot-spots' include playing fields and public playgrounds – around 180,000 children are injured annually while playing sport (ball sports being the most common cause of injury), while around 30,000 are injured at playgrounds.

Away from minor injuries, road accidents are the biggest single cause of serious injuries and death in children. In 2002, for example, around 35,000 children were hurt in accidents on the roads in the UK, with almost 5000 of these being counted as serious accidents and with 200 actual fatalities.

Surely accidents are part of growing up?

Well, yes and no. Children do need to explore their environment; only through play and trial and error do they learn which behaviours work and which don't. They also need to know how to deal with everyday risks such as crossing the road, using sharp objects or handling hot water. You cannot shield your child from every single challenge in life, and nor should you. There are also great benefits to participating in certain activities that carry a risk – sport is a good example of this, as any possible risks are outweighed by the health benefits many times over. But there is a great deal of difference between leaving children to their own devices and educating them as to how to cope with risk.

A hot drink can still scald a baby 15 minutes after it's been made.

(Source: CAPT)

The sorts of accidents that children are involved in tend to relate very closely to their age. Babies and toddlers, for example, often have accidents as a result of falling, as they have yet to develop good balance and coordination. Very young children also surprise their parents by suddenly being able to do something which the previous day they couldn't. You often hear parents in accident and emergency departments telling doctors that they turned their back for one second and their baby suddenly learned how to crawl, walk or roll into a dangerous situation. That's why accidents such as babies rolling off beds or falling down

Hot topic **Risk-prone children**

A child's personality can also have a big impact on whether they're likely to be involved in accidents. Believe it or not, some children are naturally more risk-prone or excitement-seeking than others. In fact, this tendency can even be seen in as children as young as two. In the same way that thrill-seeking adults like new and exciting situations, so risk-prone children enjoy novel and stimulating experiences and are less averse to taking physical risks. Researchers even tested to see whether babies had risk-prone personalities or not, and they discovered that babies who are quicker to react to, and reach for, new toys are more likely to go on to be toddlers who are adventurous and highly exploratory.

If you do have a child who seems to have an excitement-seeking personality, firstly, don't worry. Risk-taking children have the benefit of being highly engaged with their surroundings and can go on to lead very stimulating, fulfilling lives. The only problem is that they are also likely to be involved in accidents and take part in anti-social behaviours. As a parent, the best thing you can do is to keep a close eye on their behaviour and make sure that they understand the basics of personal safety as soon as possible. You also need to check that their risk-prone tendencies don't put their siblings or peers in danger. Try channelling their energies into positive activities such as sport or drama, which will help them to avoid potentially harmful behaviours later in life.

On a final note, children with attention deficit/hyperactivity disorder (ADHD) can also display risk-prone behaviour. This can manifest itself in the child being very impulsive, distractible and disobedient, as well as seeking out constant excitement and stimulation. If you have any concerns about your child's behaviour and suspect ADHD, talk to your family doctor.

unguarded stairs are so common. Children also lack the experience or foresight to see that a particular situation might be dangerous. *Understanding where your child is in his or her development is key to preventing accidents.*

As a parent you need to tread a careful path between allowing your child the freedom to experiment and learn while also protecting them from

Make your home safe

While it's totally impossible to shield your child from ever having an accident, you can make a significant difference to the chances of them injuring themselves at home. Consider the following:

Falls

- Install safety gates at the top and bottom of stairs until the child is a confident walker.
- Fit safety catches on windows.
- Put corner guards on tables.
- Wipe up spills and tidy up any scattered toys.
- Never leave babies unattended on raised surfaces such as beds.
- Secure loose carpets.

Burns and scalds

- Fit and regularly check smoke alarms.
- Have a fire extinguisher in the house.
- Don't smoke in the home.
- Keep matches and lighters out of reach.
- Use fireguards over gas or open fires.
- Use the back rings of the stove when cooking and turn pan handles inwards, away from the edge of the hob.
- Don't use chip pans.
- Use short or curly flexes with kettles.
- Keep hot drinks and irons away from young children.
- Set your hot water temperature lower (no more than 46°C/115°F).

Poisoning

- Keep all medicines, alcohol, essential oils, household chemicals and DIY materials out of reach and locked away.

Drowning

- Always supervise children when they are in or close to water, and never

unnecessary harm. Play and exploration are natural and highly important aspects of your child's development. By engaging with the world, children acquire crucial skills and judgement, so trying to insulate them from all risks is counter-productive in the long term. At the same time, while the odd bruise and scrape are part and parcel of being a child, you should always protect them from any unnecessary and potentially life-threatening accidents.

leave a child under five alone in a bath.

- Empty the bath immediately after use.
- Cover garden ponds and make sure water butts have lockable lids.

Cuts

- Fit safety glass in doors/windows and use safety film on glass in furniture.
- Fit safety catches on drawers.
- Keep scissors and razors out of reach.

Choking

- Supervise young children when they are eating or drinking.
- Keep small objects, such as coins and buttons, away from young children.
- Keep plastic bags and cling film out of reach.
- Follow the age recommendations on toys.

Are some children more at risk than others?

Unfortunately, the answer to this is yes. There are four main factors that affect how likely your child is to have an accident. The first is age. Children under five are the most likely to have an accident in the home, whereas this statistic declines in children between the ages of five and 15, when they are more likely to have an accident at school, at play or on the roads. The second factor is the sex of your child – boys are roughly twice as likely to have an accident as girls. The third factor is your lifestyle. Children from poorer backgrounds tend to have more accidents than children from affluent families, often because many less well-off parents lack the resources to buy important safety equipment for their home or car. And the final factor, which is closely linked to lifestyle, is physical environment. Where you live can have a big impact on child safety. If children don't have a safe place to play – as is the case with many high-rise estates or communal buildings, or where there is a large volume of traffic – accidents are commonplace.

Accident prevention

There are lots of things that you can do as a parent to reduce dramatically the likelihood of your child being involved in an accident outside the home. The

The Green Cross Code

1 Think first

Find the safest place to cross, then stop.

2 Stop

Stand on the pavement near the kerb.

3 Use your eyes and ears

Look all around for traffic, and listen.

4 Wait until it's safe to cross

If traffic is coming, let it pass.

5 Look and listen

When it's safe, walk straight across the road.

6 Arrive alive

Keep looking and listening for traffic while you cross.

statistics may seem frightening, but they do include accidents that happen as a result of parents not taking measures to protect their children from harm.

It seems obvious, but taking precautionary measures will dramatically reduce your child's chances of being in an incident. Take accidents as a result of cycling, for example. In 2003, in the UK, 18 children were killed in cycling road accidents: 577 were seriously injured and just over 4000 children suffered minor injuries. While that may seem like a lot, there are three things to bear in mind. First, many of the children who were seriously injured or died in these accidents had failed to wear a safety helmet.

The second thing to consider is that, however frightening it might feel to let your children ride a bike (and there's no doubt that most parents worry about their child when they are out cycling), the long-term health benefits for your child far outweigh any potential risk from an accident. According to the British Medical Association, the gain of 'life years' through improved fitness as a result of regular cycling exceeds the loss of 'life years' in cycle fatalities by a factor of 20 to one. Put another way, obesity and other health problems linked to a lack of exercise are 20 times more likely to kill you than a cycling accident.

The last thing to consider is that, although activities outside the home are often a cause of childhood accidents, this does not mean that children will not get injured if they are kept at home. As the statistics show, children stand an equal chance of being injured in an accident at home as outside it.

Children under eight years old

Children under eight should be supervised by an adult at all times when they are outside the home because, although children of this age are beginning to develop common sense, they are still far too young to understand many of the dangers present in the outside world. A great thing to start doing at this age is introducing the idea of potential hazards while making it into a game. That way they will be keen to spot problems before they happen. For example, it's never too early to start teaching the basics of road safety – holding your child's hand at all times, you can instruct them how to cross roads safely and practise the Green Cross Code when you are out together. After a few times you can even let them suggest safe places to cross when you are out and about.

In particular, children under eight shouldn't be allowed to cross the road by themselves, as they are still too young to be able to judge the speed and distance of traffic properly. They are also too small to see or be seen by road users. The same goes for cycling on the road, but that doesn't mean young children can't get lots of practice in the safety of the back garden or the park. However, a cycle helmet should still be worn at all times.

Children at this age also need to understand the dangers of fire and water. If you haven't already done so, take your child along to swimming lessons with a qualified instructor who will teach him or her about water safety.

Kris's Top Tips

Invest in safety equipment

To help you create a safe environment and eliminate needless risks, invest in basic pieces of child safety equipment, including child locks, fireguards, smoke alarms, stair gates, pond covers and cycle helmets. Remember that certain items of safety gear, such as safety belts and child car seats, are compulsory by law.

Teach basic safety

Show your children the ground rules both inside and outside the home, and then let them acquire experience under supervision from a responsible adult.

Who can they trust?

Encourage your child to be wary of strangers, but also teach them that in an emergency situation, or when lost or scared, they should find someone in uniform to help them out.

Keep things in proportion

Don't let worry spoil your experience of being a parent or unnecessarily limit your child's development. Worry about the real risks to your child's safety – such as road traffic, lack of exercise, domestic violence and poor diet – while keeping a sense of proportion about random risks such as murder and abduction.

Set a good example

If you want your children to be safety-conscious, set a good example both at home and when you are out and about. Lots of parents lecture children about road safety, for example, but then don't follow the basic rules themselves.

Get involved with the school

Your child will spend a large proportion of their time away from you at school, so you need to feel reassured that it is a place that takes child safety seriously. Ask about the school's written safety and bullying policies, and encourage them to host child safety courses such as cycling proficiency and the Green Cross Code.

Think about your child's personality

Don't underestimate your child's natural tendencies – if they have a risk-seeking personality, you will need to channel their energies into positive physical pursuits.

Do a first-aid course

Even in the safest of environments, children have an uncanny knack of finding danger. If the worst should ever happen, you'll be better prepared if you've taken a child first-aid course. Your local surgery should have details of courses near you.

Ask where, who and when

Older children will expect some degree of freedom when away from home. To keep them safe, try to ensure that you always know where your child is, who they are with and when they'll be back. Get them to give you a contact telephone number if they can, or consider providing them with a mobile phone for emergencies.

Teach your child 999

If your children get into trouble while away from home, make sure they always know that they can dial 999 in an emergency. There is also a second emergency number, 112.

NB – These numbers should be used only if life is threatened, someone is injured or you suspect that a crime has been committed.

Children aged seven to 11

The period between the ages of seven and 11 is a prime time for road accidents involving children. By this age they will probably be keen to walk short distances by themselves, so let your child plan safe routes to school and other nearby destinations. This will encourage them to make decisions and take responsibility for their own safety, and you can help them along by inviting them to talk about what is safe and dangerous on the roads.

At this age, your child might also want to start cycling by themselves. If this is the case, try to get them to take a cycling proficiency course. It is probably still too early for your child to be cycling on busy roads unsupervised, but you can help them find safe places for cycling, away from traffic, while they build up their road sense. Make sure they are wearing a helmet and reflective clothing at all times.

chapter 10

Communication

The way we interact with our children makes a huge difference to their happiness and confidence as adults. Communication and emotional intelligence are particularly important. Interacting with your child is about how you communicate with them – and about teaching them these skills that will be so important to them as they grow up.

Communicating with your child

The older they get, the more inclined children become to withhold information from their parents – whether it's about practical matters, such as what's happening at school, or emotional issues, such as sex and confidence. The process is natural and healthy: it's how they begin to make discoveries and experiment with their newfound independence.

But the word 'experiment' is key here. By definition, experimentation means sometimes not getting it right, and this can occur during the times when children retreat too far away from their parents simply to 'see what happens'. There are things you can do if this situation arises, but the most important is to keep calm and accept that it's a natural part of growing up, and they are just seeing how it feels to be self-reliant. If you stay calm and don't overreact to a situation, your children are much more likely to come back to you when they realize your advice and support are valuable and important to them.

Emotional intelligence ('EI')

Until very recently, psychologists viewed intelligence strictly in terms of simple abilities such as verbal, numerical and spatial skills. However, this view completely ignored one of the most important aspects of intelligence that humans have – the ability to understand emotions in both ourselves and in others.

Emotional intelligence (EI) began as a theory of psychology in the early 1990s, so it's a relatively new concept, but an incredibly important one. Put simply, it means how good we are at understanding our emotions and those of others, and the level of subtlety and complexity we use to do this. For example, most of us can spot when someone is feeling angry, but how many of us can tell when that anger is hiding something else – such as fear, sadness or worry?

The kinds of abilities that would be counted under emotional intelligence are as follows:

Sensitivity
Awareness of someone else's moods and feelings.

Understanding

The ability to understand someone else's problems (even if you haven't experienced them yourself), and communicate this to that person.

Empathy

Being able to put yourself in someone else's shoes.

Sympathy

Being caring and gentle when someone is upset or troubled.

Anticipation

Being able to predict how an event or a discussion will affect somebody, based on their personality and experiences.

Diplomacy

Handling a difficult problem or subject in a way that least upsets somebody else.

Timing

Being able to judge when it is a good time for someone to hear something difficult or upsetting.

'Normal' intelligence (verbal, numerical and so on) is something that can be developed through practice, good teaching and exposure to lots of different problems and the methods for solving them. Emotional intelligence is exactly the same – as we broaden our mind, so we can also broaden our EI.

Our EI develops and grows constantly throughout our life. Infants understand little about emotions, but by the time they're about three they can recognize the most common ones. A big change, of course, occurs during puberty, when children begin to experience lots of totally new emotions that they never knew existed. It's no wonder puberty can be such a difficult and confusing time.

Even into adulthood we are gaining new emotional intelligence as we are exposed to new emotions. Grief, for example, is something that many of us may not fully experience until middle age, when for the first time someone close to us dies. Over the course of that loss, and for months or even years afterwards, we gain some completely new EI that wasn't there before.

Why EI is important for parents

Using emotional intelligence is important right from birth. Parents have to learn very quickly to recognize emotions in their babies – pain, fear and hunger being the obvious ones. When things are going well, of course, other emotions that our babies express, such as contentment and excitement, can bring us great joy and satisfaction.

As babies become toddlers, their 'emotional range' expands – frustration and anger appear, as well as puzzlement and fascination. When toddlers learn to talk, our understanding of our children's emotions is given a big boost, because they will tell us exactly how they're feeling. But as communication is improving, so is the complexity of our children's emotions. With puberty, as we'll see later, come changes that make it hard for children to explain how they're feeling, and even harder for us parents to work it out for ourselves.

Having confidence in your EI

In previous chapters, I've talked about the negative labels we give to ourselves and to our children, and what we are actually capable of. We might say that we weren't very bright at school, or that we're just 'not very sporty', and nine times out of ten these labels are nonsense – they're just a sign that we've never gained confidence in that particular activity.

Emotional intelligence is exactly the same. You often meet people who say they're not very good with emotions, or 'just not very sensitive'. This is simply untrue. Everybody has emotions, everybody has the ability to understand them in others, and everybody has the ability to develop and improve their EI. The only people for whom this isn't the case are those suffering from rare medical conditions such as autism or Asperger's syndrome.

This doesn't necessarily mean when someone says they're not very good with emotions that it's a cop-out or some kind of emotional laziness. Just like academic performance or sport, early bad experiences or a lack of support from our own parents or loved ones can shake our confidence in an ability and, as with sport or academia, this can cause some people to give up trying to understand others, or be sensitive to or empathize with them.

All children need understanding – it's too important to give up on. By the same token, have confidence in your children's emotional intelligence and don't underestimate their ability to understand complicated emotions. Just as with normal intelligence, the idea should be to 'stretch' your children's emotional understanding constantly. A great number of parents feel it is their duty to protect their children from all emotional upset, but really the opposite is true. You need to expose your children to emotional issues in such a way that they'll be able to handle them, learn from them and grow stronger as they get older. Children who reach adolescence without any real emotional experience may find themselves in emotional situations later on that they struggle to cope with.

Being an emotional role model

When children are growing up and struggling to get to grips with their own emotions and those of others, they look to us to help them to understand these feelings, but also to see how to behave in certain situations.

Being a good emotional role model for your children will teach them vital skills for later life – in work, in relationships, and for when they themselves become parents. In a way, you should see yourself as part of a cycle: the lessons you teach your children now about dealing with feelings are very likely to be copied by them when they have children. It may be that your parents weren't very sensitive or understanding with you, but you have the power to break that cycle, and to teach your children a better way of doing things.

Understanding your child

Emotional intelligence requires the understanding of certain key principles. One of these is the principle that everyone is different – not just in their tastes, interests and academic ability, but in their personality and temperament. You can't be emotionally intelligent without using this as a guiding principle for the way in which to conduct relationships with others. In parenthood, this idea that we're different is crucial. Your children are different from...

...You

Although they share your genes, in personality and in temperament children are often very different from either or both parents. They are also growing up in a world that is far removed from the one you grew up in, and this will influence their personality in a big way.

...Their siblings

Variation in personality between siblings is caused by an assortment of things, including birth order and early experiences such as illnesses, unusual talents or disabilities.

...Their friends

This sounds obvious enough – after all, there's no reason why two children from different families should have anything in common – but the reasons why children choose their particular friends are complex. Sometimes they pick a friend because they are like them, but sometimes it is for the opposite reason – because they are different and therefore interesting. Romantic relationships are just as unpredictable, and we rarely fall in love with someone who is identical to us in every way.

When many parents have their first child they believe that they are a sort of 'blank canvas' and that, with the right parenting, they'll become exactly what the parents would like them to be – clever, confident, well-behaved and so on. It's usually after the second child arrives that parents realize how much of their children's personality is 'innate' and not necessarily to do with the environment in which they grow up. Two children raised in exactly the same way will often turn out to be completely different: one might be outgoing, the other shy; one might perform brilliantly at school, whereas the other might find it a struggle.

From your point of view, the important thing is to get to know your child's unique temperament, accept it (rather than try to alter it) and then change the way you deal with them accordingly – especially when they're very young. This principle works for all sorts of things, such as taking your child for their first day at school. If they are confident and sociable, let them run off and play with their friends as soon as they get there; but if they're shy, don't push them away – instead comfort them as much as possible and take time to persuade them why they'll enjoy being at school.

Many parents find this a difficult principle to put into practice because they don't want to be seen to treat their children differently; they worry that if they're inconsistent, one or both children might accuse them of favouritism. The way to deal with this is to explain to them the point that we've made here – that everyone is different, with different needs, personality and so on.

None of this means that there aren't principles of good parenting that will apply regardless of your child's temperament, but it's how you put those principles into practice with each child that counts.

Communication

Imagine a teacher in a classroom taking an important lesson with a class of children. Imagine the teacher just sitting there and saying nothing for the whole 45 minutes. The children wouldn't learn much, would they?

Now imagine a second classroom. In this one, the teacher talks almost constantly for the 45 minutes, full of interesting information, speaking in a lively and clear style, but at the end of the lesson the teacher asks the class a question only to find that 90 per cent of the children stopped paying attention long ago. They've learned more than they did in the first classroom, but not much more.

Finally, imagine a third classroom. The teacher in this classroom is also lively and clear, but as well as that, this teacher does something else: he asks questions of the pupils constantly, he listens to what they say, and then he tells them what he thinks. The lesson is more like a discussion than a lecture, and so the pupils learn far more because they feel as though their opinions are important, as well as the teacher's.

A two-way process

You'll very likely have heard this saying before: that *communication is a two-way process*. It's an idea that the majority of us would agree with, but agreeing with it and putting it into practice are very, very different things. Nowhere in life is practising two-way communication harder than in parenthood – but why is this so?

Parenting is full of pitfalls and traps. In the tough times it can feel as though being a parent is like a test, in which someone is trying to catch you out at every possible opportunity. One of the biggest traps comes from being in a position of authority. Although you have the power (which might feel like a good thing), you also have the responsibility, the hard work, the worry and the guilt, while your children have the happy, fun-filled childhood that you're desperately trying to create for them.

Another common trap parents fall into is *knowing better than your child*. We could talk about the 'wisdom of youth' until the cows came home, but for their earlier childhood at least, you will have a better idea of how to handle a situation than they will. So, as we all feel from time to time, why bother communicating with our children about how and why something needs to get done? Surely we should just get on and do it as quickly and efficiently as possible? After all, ultimately the final decision will be made by us as parents anyway.

The reason we fall into both of these traps is that we forget the main aim of parenting. It isn't to do everything for your child, such as:

- Ferry them round like royalty.
- Protect them from all possible dangers.
- Make sure they get good results at school, even if it means doing the work for them.

The main aim of parenting is to teach.

As a parent you are a kind of teacher on a constant basis: this other role involves teaching your children how to interact with others, how to take responsibility, how to overcome difficulties and so on. In so much of what we do with our children, it's not whether or not the outcome is successful, it's how much they've learned along the way – *and they won't learn anything unless you communicate with them patiently and clearly.*

Let's look at communication from another angle. What can be affected if parents don't communicate properly with their children?

Learning

Parents need to teach their children all sorts of things throughout their life, from discipline and boundaries to how to manage their money and to emotional issues. If you can't communicate with your children, this learning simply can't take place.

Mutual understanding

Your understanding of your children, and their understanding of you, depends enormously on regular, clear and open communication. There is so much that you need to know about each other, and this need doesn't lessen the more time you spend together. Parents and children who don't communicate can find that they don't know each other at all.

Trust

It's vital that your children trust you, and this comes in part as a result of your ability to communicate with them: it's very difficult to trust someone if you don't understand what they're saying to you.

Emotional support

Your children will need your emotional support throughout their life. They'll need to feel that they can come to you and talk about anything that is bothering them without you dismissing what they say, being impatient because you don't understand, or flying off the handle if they've got themselves into trouble. None of this will be possible unless you can communicate with them.

Direction

By this we mean 'guidance', and this relates to all sorts of things. Children who stop talking or listening to their parents are the ones who are most likely to get into trouble or stop living up to their potential. They are also the ones who are more likely to feel unloved and insecure, leading to unhappiness and a loss of confidence.

Listening

The key to successful communication is *listening*, and this is all the more important for people who are in a position of authority. The most successful leaders and managers, and the ones who are most successful at maintaining their authority, are those who really listen to what their staff have to say.

It's just the same for parents. You are a leader – the leader of a family – and your children will quickly lose faith in your leadership if they don't feel that you listen to them enough. Many parents tend to think of parenting as an exercise in conveying information and instructions to their children, and these are often the same parents who complain that their children never tell them anything. But why should they tell us anything if we don't listen to what they have to say?

There's a very simple rule of thumb that you can follow here: in any conversation with a child, you should each be talking for 50 per cent of the time. It doesn't matter whether you know more about something than your child, or if you have started the conversation and it's about something that you have to tell them – you should still be listening for 50 per cent of the time. If you don't listen, you'll have no way of knowing whether they've understood you.

So we know that conversations should be as equal as possible: now for the really important bit. We might have the right intentions and know that we ought to listen, but many parents think this simply means 'letting your child have a say' or, effectively, allowing enough silences in your own speech to allow them to talk. This is important, of course, but it's only a small part of what listening is really about.

Remember: *listening is about taking a genuine interest in what someone is saying*. Your child could babble away for hours, but unless you're actually listening to and thinking about what they say, it might as well be wasted time.

We all get into conversations with other adults in which we can tell that they're not really interested in what we're saying – whether it's at work, in a shop, or with friends and relatives – but the ability to notice this is not just restricted to adults. Don't forget that, from a very early age, children pick up on this too. Don't kid yourself that you can pretend to listen while in fact you're wondering whether you set the video, or thinking about that important meeting tomorrow.

Three out of four children aged between 11 and 16 say that 'being listened to' is the thing that determines how happy they are about their relationship with their parents.

Tips for how to be a good listener

Leave silences in a conversation from time to time – silence gives children the opportunity to talk about something on their own terms. This is often true of really important issues, such as emotional problems.

Ask open questions

This means questions that can't be answered with a 'yes', 'no' or 'don't know'. Ask questions that require detail and explanations.

You don't have to agree with everything

The important thing is that you've listened to what your child says, and thought about it. You've shown that you respect them. After that, it's OK to explain why you don't agree with something they've said – as long as you give good reasons.

Don't stop communicating when things are going well

Good communication is a habit, like keeping a tidy home or eating healthily. You need to keep the habit going all the time and that way, if a problem does arise, your child will find it easier to talk to you.

Switch off the TV while talking
The same applies to all sorts of distractions, such as doing chores or looking after another child. Make an effort to give your child your time and your complete attention.

As often as possible, keep an open mind
You can't always change decisions on your child's say so but, wherever possible, be willing and ready to change a decision if your child gives you genuine reasons as to why you should.

Finally, a quick point about starting conversations. When we get home from work, the last thing we want to talk about is work, so why should children be any different about school? If you're starting a conversation, choose something your child will be interested in. Begin with something that will engage their interest, such as friends or hobbies – it's much easier to talk to a child about something mundane (like schoolwork) once they've already had a fun conversation about music or fashion.

Communicating with older children
We all know the cliché about teenagers – on the day of their thirteenth birthday they magically transform from angelic, doting cherubs into something resembling a junior member of the Hell's Angels. Disrespectful, messy, disorganized, lazy and – worst of all – uncommunicative.

Is this cliché about how teens develop really the way things are? If you've got teenagers already you'll have your own ideas, but research suggests that there's at least an element of truth about it, as reported by both teens and their parents.

Many parents notice a significant drop in communication with their children some time during the early teens. There is a number of reasons as to why this takes place, but there's one that dwarfs the others – puberty. Here's why puberty has such a strong impact on teenagers and the way they communicate, as well as what you can do to help:

Recalling your own teenage years

If you have children who are approaching their teens, all these changes might sound frankly terrifying. Well, for children it certainly can be. But, as with many stressful events that we face in our life, the best thing we can do to stay calm is to familiarize ourselves before the event with what is going to happen.

Take some time to recall your own teenage years. Do as many of the following as you can over a period of a weeks:

Memories

Remember everything you can about being a 13-year-old – where you were, your friends, your school and your hobbies. Some memories might be more painful than others, but persevere, because it will give you valuable insight into what your children are going through.

Personal items

Schoolbooks, music and old clothes (if you still have them) are great for prompting reminiscences about your teenage life.

Talk to family and friends

Ask your parents what they remember about your teenage years – everything from your personality to physical changes.

Speak to other parents

Other parents are great to talk to because they went through their teenage years at a similar time to you, and they may even have teenage children now.

Physical changes

The physical changes that occur during puberty are genuinely upsetting and strange for many children and in some cases can lead to mild depression and 'cutting off' from others.

Embarrassment can be key here, and this is often misread by parents. So give your children privacy and personal space wherever possible. Offer advice (generally better received from the parent of the same sex), but don't pressure them to take it as this can make things worse rather than better. Finally, teach your children to be proud of and comfortable with their body before they reach their teenage years, and warn them that changes will happen so that it's not a shock when the time comes.

Romantic and sexual feelings

Like physical changes, new-found romantic or sexual feelings can be confusing, scary and embarrassing. The same advice applies here as above – give them space and take the opportunity, if it's presented, to reassure your child that their feelings are natural and healthy. Don't make fun of them under any circumstances.

Personality changes

The 'split personality' cliché about teen-agers does hold true in some cases. Hor-

Almost half of all teenagers say that they feel unable to discuss problems with their parents. The most common time for these communication problems to appear is between the ages of 12 and 13. The problem tends to be worse for boys than girls, but children of all ages say they are more likely to talk to their mother than their father.

monal and physical changes can cause major, unpredictable changes in a child's temperament, personality and moods. It's because the personality is heavily influenced by the chemistry of the brain. This can be extremely puzzling for parents, especially if you yourself had a fairly easy time of it when you were a teenager. As for your child, puberty can create totally new feelings of anxiety, depression, hyperactivity and many other things. Their natural reaction to this can be to cut themselves off for fear of losing control in front of their family or others. The best approach for adults here is to listen, and take whatever your teenagers say about how they're feeling seriously.

You might think that your children are also responsible for communicating, and surely if they cut off from you, that doesn't mean it's your fault… Well, as children get older and have to take responsibility for all sorts of things, they do need to take greater responsibility for communication – with parents, teachers and friends to name just a few. And yes, if your child does cut off from you suddenly (very often in adolescence), it doesn't necessarily mean you're to blame, or that you could have seen it coming and prevented it.

There are all sorts of other reasons why children, and particularly adolescents, 'cut off' like this. For some it's a case of exploring independence and emotional distance from their parents, whereas for others it's about enjoying the first experience of privacy. There is, of course, one other sadly common reason, too – bullying.

Bullying

If you are worried that your child is being bullied, ask them directly. Children are often frightened to talk about what is happening, so be prepared for your child to deny that there is anything wrong at first. Encourage them to talk to you by saying that you are concerned and you want to help and support them, whatever the problem. Take whatever they say seriously, and try to find out exactly what has been going on. Don't promise to keep the bullying secret, but do reassure them that the more they tell you, the more you'll be able to sort out the problem.

In 2000, research involving 2300 pupils aged 10–14 from schools across England found that 30 per cent of children did not tell anyone that they had been bullied. This percentage was higher for boys and older children.

Kris's Top Tips

■ Develop and have confidence in your own emotional intelligence, even if you don't think understanding and sensitivity are your strong points.

■ Understanding your child's unique personality is vital, but remember that children's personalities are constantly changing and they may show different sides to themselves when they're not in your company.

■ Remember what it was like to be a teenager, and how difficult it can be. Use your past experiences to guide how you communicate with your children when they are that age.

■ If your children 'cut off' from you at any point, there are all sorts of possible reasons. Don't assume the worst, and don't discount the possibility that your child is simply anxious or embarrassed about something.

■ Communication is a two-way process. Within any one conversation with your child, you should be aiming to talk for 50 per cent of the time and listen for the other 50 per cent – even if you're trying to communicate a set of instructions. It's harder than it sounds, but keep practising and don't give up.

■ Don't forget that parenting isn't just about the end result – it's about what your children learn along the way. They won't learn anything unless you communicate with them constantly.

■ Parenting isn't about sheltering your children: they should be exposed to emotional events as soon as they are able to understand them. It will give them experience, a sense of responsibility and strength in the future.

■ Remember how important it is to be a good role model for your children when it comes to emotions, feelings and communication. The behaviour you're teaching them now will influence them for the rest of their life.

■ Talk to other parents and your children's friends and teachers – they can often give you other perspectives and fill in the gaps about things your children aren't telling you.

Further resources

ACAS helpline
Tel: 08457 474747

ADDISS (Attention Deficit Disorder Information and Support Service)
Tel: 0208 906 9068
www.addiss.co.uk

BBC websites
www.bbc.co.uk/bbcthree/tv/killing_the_kids
www.bbc.co.uk/health
www.bbc.co.uk/parenting
http://www.bbc.co.uk/skillswise/tutors/
expertcolumn/dyscalculia

British Dyslexia Association (BDA)
Tel: 0118 966 8271
www.bda-dyslexia.co.uk

Bullying Online
www.bullying.co.uk

Child Alert
www.childalert.co.uk

Child Poverty Action Group
94 White Lion Street
London N1 9PF
Tel: 0207 837 7979
www.cpag.org.uk

Department for Education
Tel: 0870 000 2288
www.dfes.gov.uk

Department of Health
Tel: 0207 210 4850
www.dh.gov.uk/Home/fs/en

Department of Transport – Road Safety Advice
www.hedgehogs.gov.uk

Dyscalculia
www.bbc.co.uk/skillswise/tutors/
expertcolumn/dyscalculia

Feed Me Better Campaign: Jamie's School Dinners
www.feedmebetter.com

Food Standards Agency
Tel: 0207 276 8000
www.food.gov.uk

House of Tiny Tearaways by Dr Tanya Byron, BBC Books, London 2005

Little Angels, by Dr Tanya Byron and Sacha Baveystock, BBC Books, London 2005

Medical Research Council
Tel: 0207 636 5422
www.mrc.ac.uk

My Sport
www.trymysport.co.uk

NSPCC
Tel: 0207 825 2500
www.nspcc.org.uk

Parents' Centre
www.parentscentre.gov.uk

Parents' Line
www.parentlineplus.org.uk

Sport England
www.activeplaces.com

UK Government
www.direct.gov.uk/Parents

World Health Organization
www.who.int/en/

Acknowledgements

To my gorgeous three kids who show me what works (and what doesn't!) and my ever-patient and loving husband. Also to my mum and dad, who taught me everything I know about parenting.

Special thanks to my highly supportive partners at the innovation company ?What If! and everyone who has worked on the programme; and in particular to Robin Ashbrook, Dympna Jackson and Elisabeth Bayliffe for taking a chance on me!

Thanks also to Sally and Alistair Bevan, for all their fantastic research and help with the book, and to Emma Shackleton for spotting the potential of the programme and transcribing it into a book to help parents.

BBC Active would like to thank Jon Tonks, Billie-Jo Boyd, Olivia Hall, Nicholas Ivanov, Jordan Smith, Peter Wilding, and James and Joe.

All photographs: ChrisCapstick © BBC Active.

Index